TAKING CHARGE
Of Organizational Conflict

A Guide to Managing Anger and Confrontation

David Cowan

PERSONHOOD PRESS • Fawnskin, California

cover design: Doug Armstrong
cover photograph: Robert Cowen
editor: Dianne Schilling

Printed in United States of America

For information address:
Personhood Press
"Books for ALL that you are!"
Post Office Box 370
Fawnskin, California 92333
800.662.9662   e-mail: personhoodpress@att.net

Library of Congress Cataloging-in-publication Data:
David Cowan, 1944

Taking Charge of Organizational Conflict (Revised and Expanded) / by David Cowan

ISBN: 1-932181-011-3

Original version published as Taking Charge of Organizational Conflict
by David Cowan, Innerchoice Publishing, 1995

Visit our Web site at —
http://www.personhoodpress.com

Visit David Cowan's Web site at —
www.davecowan.com

Dedication

To Tom Pettepiece, a dear friend, a guide
and an inspiration forever.

In the past,
people thought they could
fight wars in far off lands,
or know children were dying from hunger,
or not sit next to a person with
different colored skin,
and still be at peace within themselves.
The search for inner peace and the progress toward
social justice
were separate worlds.

Now we understand
that we are not truly at peace
within ourselves
if our neighbor's life is crumbling,
whether they are someone
we know personally
or only a face on television.

Peace is not another alternative,
theory, or theology,
but a new choice
for the mainstream of life.
Peace does not look forward
to a future golden age.
It simply is.
Now.

Thomas Pettepiece
What Everybody Already Knows:
A Book About Peacemaking

TAKING CHARGE OF
ORGANIZATIONAL CONFLICT

CONTENTS

I .... *APPROACHES TO CONFRONTATION — QUICK REFERENCE*

III ...... *CONFLICT MANAGEMENT STRATEGIES — QUICK REFERENCE*

1 .... INTRODUCTION **1.**
About Taking Charge of Organizational Conflict
Civility and Getting Along
Deadly Assumptions
People Drive Everything
Mechanics of Conflict Management
The Possibilities of Conflict

11 .... THE SOURCES OF CONFLICT **2.**

23 .... DYNAMICS OF CONFLICT **3.**
Unmanaged Conflict Equals Destructive Consequences
From Disagreement to Crisis
Win-Lose and Lose-Lose
Managed Conflict Equals Positive Change and
Personal Growth
The Win-Win Outcome
Connecting Conflict to Productivity
Better Conflict Management Means Resource Conservation
Consequences of Personal and Professional Conflict
The Evolution of Conflict
The Impact of Crisis

69 .... THE NATURE OF CONFLICT **4.**
Diversity and Conflict
Comfort Zones and Conflict
Conflict and Stress
Mindworks, Stress, and Conflict
Action versus Reaction
The Gateway Skill

103 .... DIALOGUE HOLDS THE KEY **5.**
A Medium for Dialogue
Increasing Awareness
Achieving Mastery
Listening — The Master Skill
Listening Is Situational
Barriers to Listening
Listening Out Loud
Conflict Connection

119 .... MANAGING CONFRONTATIONS **6.**
First Aid Fast
First Aid for Intrapersonal Conflict
Special Confrontations
Handling Difficult People

145 .... CONFLICT STRATEGIES **7.**
Problem Solving
Communicating Strategically
Developing the Use of "I" Messages

173 .... THE ART & SCIENCE OF MEDIATION **8.**
In The Middle
How To Mediate a Conflict
Mechanics of Mediation
Benefits of Conflict Mediation

187 .... IMPORTANT PROCESSES **9.**
Group Work Circles
Comprehensive Feedback Model

See Page 127 **Expect Expectations** — Most people engaging in confrontation or conflict do so with preconceptions or expectations. Anticipating and coming to understand these expectations provides an excellent place to begin diffusing and disarming a confrontation.

See Page 127 **Put Them First** — Most of the time when confrontation or conflict arises we are occupied with other tasks. The natural temptation is to subordinate conflict or confrontation to the task at hand. Don't! Put the person or persons you're dealing with in any confrontation in a priority position. This is crucial!

See Page 128 **Prepare a Place and Keep It Holy** — Among the easiest things you can do is to prepare a place in which to accommodate confrontive situations. The impact of a relaxed, peaceful, safe place is often enough to disarm a difficult situation.

See Page 129 **Are You Listening?** Because of the emotional nature of both confrontation and conflict, first-aid listening requires conscious awareness and control. Here are the tips you can use to restore equilibrium to a confrontive situation.

See Page 129 **Move From Right to Left** — Taking the wind out of the emotional side of a confrontation lets you begin to focus on the more substantive issues whether they involve tangible things or personal values.

See Page 130 **Absorbing Energy** — Aside from the conscious tools we can employ to diffuse and disarm confrontation, there are a number of behaviors that we can exhibit in confrontive situations that go far to absorb the high levels of energy people bring to them.

See Page 131   **Getting to Want** — Whatever obvious things people want from confrontive encounters, or no matter how much altruism or objectivity may appear in their arguments, be assured that everyone is also operating from some level of self-interest. These accumulated "wants" are primary motivators in confrontation. Understanding and clarifying wants is vital to achieving desirable outcomes.

See Page 132   **What Can I Do?** This is perhaps the most important question you can ask. It slices to the issues by approaching them from the results end rather than focusing on causes or blame.

See Page 132   **What I Will Do** — By providing immediate and clear actions aimed at the concerns of those involved in either confrontation or conflict, we begin the discovery process that leads to resolution.

See Page 133   **Mea Culpa** — Though it sounds simple, most of us find it difficult to apologize. This is a powerful means of setting the stage for meaningful discussion of problems and issues. It lets others know we are assuming a measure of responsibility in bringing about solution or resolution.

See Page 133   **Neutralize and Reduce Resistance** — Here are some specific little things you can do to break through resistance that exists when people are emotionally attached either to an issue or an expectation. This is how you create alignment around the management and ultimate resolution of conflicts.

See Page 134   **Do Your Homework** — Not only is this an outstanding prevention tool, it is a great way to determine the extent of a problem. Very often, we only see the tip of the iceberg when we are presented with a confrontation. When the confrontation articulates a symptom of a greater problem, this tool allows us to get to the cause.

See Page 135   **Don't Be Part of the Problem** — What we bring to a confrontation or conflict will have some effect . . . make sure it's positive.

See Page 152	**1. Abandoning**
See Page 153	**2. Avoiding**
See Page 155	**3. Dominating**
See Page 155	**4. Obliging**
See Page 156	**5. Getting Help**
See Page 158	**6. Humor**
See Page 158	**7. Postponing**
See Page 160	**8. Compromise**
See Page 160	**9. Integrating**
See Page 162	**10. Collaboration**

INTRODUCTION

1.

TAKING CHARGE OF
ORGANIZATIONAL CONFLICT

1. INTRODUCTION

Just What Business Are You In?

Most people involved in organizational leadership have a pretty good grasp of the fact that the incidence of conflict is increasing or, at least, that conflict often gets in the way of getting things done.

Conflict includes everything from simple disagreements to outright violence. Moreover, it goes far beyond the interpersonal conflicts in which we and the people around us tend to become involved. It also includes those countless mental and emotional struggles that we deal with at a personal level.

> If we want more peace, we must have less conflict — be in conflict less of the time, which is not to say eliminate conflict, but is to say manage and resolve it better.

Like interpersonal conflicts, internal, or intrapersonal, conflicts also vary in degree and mostly have to do with decisions and distress. Take a moment and consider the process of coming to a decision. At its simplest, it's merely choice-making. But choices range from easy ones, like what to eat for lunch, to absorbing ones, like who in an organization is going to be reassigned or laid off when budgets are cut.

It seems reasonable to conclude that whenever a business spends a significant portion of its resources in a particular pursuit, that pursuit is part of what the organization is in business to do.

Together, internal and interpersonal conflicts consume so much time and attention that some organizations start to look as though conflict is their primary business.

Are you investing so much time and energy in conflict in your life or your organization that it's starting to look as though you are in the conflict business?

My experience in dealing with all kinds of organizations; big and small, public and private, and for profit and nonprofit, leads me to believe that, more and more, organizations are in the conflict business — not by choice, but certainly to the detriment of almost everything else they are trying to accomplish.

More good intentions, well-conceived programs, personal and organizational vitality, and potentially productive careers lie dead on the road because of poorly managed conflict and its potentially hideous consequences than due to any other ill facing organizations today.

This being the case, it appears that in the management of conflict a wonderful opportunity exists to enhance effectiveness and productivity while deepening commitment to the human side of the organization.

Examine your own organization and ask yourself if you don't agree that, based on what you see, you are more in the conflict business than you previously thought. If the answer is yes, this book is for you.

ABOUT THIS BOOK

Taking Charge of Organizational Conflict is written to help you come to grips with all kinds of conflicts. A popular myth says that if your department or business is experiencing conflict, it's because management isn't doing its job. But, if you and the people around you are engaged in any activity at all, at some point you are going to become involved in conflict. It's normal and it's going to happen. The key to your success in these situations is to effectively and productively manage and take advantage of conflict. The overriding purpose of this book is to help you forge and use such a key.

Achieving an understanding of the conditions that tend to generate conflict as well as the effects or dynamics of conflict is vital. When these understandings are grounded in theory, you are better prepared to comprehend what goes on in a conflict situation and better able to take charge. The book is organized to provide these insights and then to build a solid base for managing and taking command of situations ranging from simple confrontations to crises.

CIVILITY AND GETTING ALONG

What does it take for people to get along? What is required for individuals and groups from diverse backgrounds to willingly seek common ground while maintaining respect for the things they bring to the places they share?

Looking at the configurations of people in organizations, we find microcosms of our multicultural society — a society made up almost exclusively of immigrants and the descendents of immigrants or those who, for whatever other reasons, now find themselves part of this amazing diversity. For whatever reasons and by whatever circumstances we have come to a particular organization, we must develop a set of ethics and skills that enable us to appreciate and then take advantage of the wonderful kaleidoscope of colors and cultures we have inherited.

We can start by recognizing that any organization possesses dynamics of civility similar to those of the society as a whole. One difference is that maintaining civility and getting along are far more easily accomplished on this smaller scale. Getting along does not mean the absence of conflict, but rather implies our ability to manage conflict in ways that produce higher levels of harmony and productivity.

Merely admonishing people to be "good citizens" is not enough. Everyone is familiar with this label and can parrot all of its implied expectations. For individuals to get along in the spirit of true interdependence, they have to develop self-awareness; undertake responsibility for their actions; accept and appreciate differences in others; listen with empathy and understanding; communicate their thoughts and feelings accurately and assertively; include others in their activities; be open to divergent styles and points of view; work together to solve problems and complete projects; and peacefully resolve the myriads of conflicts they encounter and experience along the way.

To do all this is no small undertaking, but neither is it as daunting a task as it may seem. It does require effort directed at creating necessary awarenesses and understandings, and then it demands focus by the organization and all its people.

What this book offers is an information base and a set of structures designed to equip you with the only additional resources you need to redirect a major portion of the time, energy, and other resources currently being squandered on knee-jerk reactions and other inappropriate and ineffective responses to conflict.

Taking Charge of Organizational Conflict is not the complete answer, but it is a great place to start. If you marry what you find here with almost any degree of appropriate effort, the payoffs will be enormous.

DEADLY ASSUMPTIONS

As we prepare people to be successful in the workplace, we tend to think primarily about the skills they must possess in order to accomplish a particular job. We get people ready by giving them tools they need to be successful and to contribute. However, we very often assume that people are better able and more willing to perform than they really are.

> In selecting people, Hardly ever do we assess or even consider a persons ability to manage conflict.

In today's organizations, it is not enough to have job-related skills. It has become vitally important for people to acquire the skills necessary to successfully interact with others and to positively influence organizational culture. Too often we assume employees already possess these skills when, in fact, they don't. As we screen people for positions, we have many ways of objectively assessing job-specific skills. When we find that an individual is deficient in a certain area, we either provide training or we select a better qualified candidate. In assessing interpersonal skills, we rely almost exclusively on subjective judgement. Hardly ever do we assess or even consider a person's ability to manage conflict.

We assume that, along the way, people have adequately developed the skills necessary to resolve disputes and settle arguments. In the case of most people, nothing could be farther from the truth.

Given its importance to personal and organizational well being, the issue of conflict management should never be carelessly dismissed. Taking for granted that the average person can manage conflict, even passably, involves assumptions that individuals and organizations can no longer afford to make.

PEOPLE DRIVE EVERYTHING

We often speak of the successes or failures of organizations, but fail to remember that organizations are only structures into which we place people to produce outcomes. Any success or failure we assign to an organization is only the reflection of the success or failures of its people. People drive everything in an organization, including conflict. Understanding that it is both unwise and unsafe to assume that people are adequately prepared to deal with conflict, we must heed the counsel of Henry Ford, who said, "Before everything else, getting ready is the secret to success."

Taking Charge of Organizational Conflict is about getting ready. It is a guide to creating awareness concerning the skills that individuals and organizations must have in order to effectively manage confrontations and resolve conflicts.

MECHANICS OF CONFLICT MANAGEMENT

Conflict is the natural process by which we mediate all of our differences. The mechanics involved in managing conflict are the tools that we use to turn a perfectly natural event (a conflict) into a positive and growth-producing outcome.

> Before everything else, getting ready is the secret of success.
>
> *Henry Ford*

The difference between a well-managed and a poorly-managed conflict is a function of how we respond — of whether we act or react to the conflict, and of what skills and strategies we employ in the process.

The ultimate purpose of *Taking Charge of Organizational Conflict* is to help the reader see conflict situations for what they are and bring to bear appropriate responses. Achieving this outcome depends to a great extent on our willingness to master the mechanics of managing conflict as they are presented in the following sections.

A word of advice: Don't wait to practice the management of conflict until you find yourself or your organization in a challenging conflict situation. Consider the metaphor of a live theater production: A cast and a director work together to create an event that will please and entertain the audience and will cause everyone involved to feel proud. When you buy tickets to this play, you see the final product. You probably give little thought to the enormous effort that went into its creation — all the rehearsals, staging, costuming, etc. All the practice and preparation combine to produce an outstanding performance. Likewise, for conflict productions to have outstanding results requires enormous effort directed at practice and preparation. Don't wait until the curtain rises to begin your preparations — get ready now.

> Don't wait until the day of the game to begin your practice — you'll lose every time.

THE POSSIBILITIES OF CONFLICT

When resources are scarce, most organizations attempt to generate new avenues for securing them. When this is not possible, organizations look inward and try to conserve, as well as to increase levels of productivity from existing resources.

When we examine the negative results of poorly managed or unmanaged conflict, we see resources squandered on unproductive if not counterproductive activities. On the other hand, when conflict is well managed and dealt with effectively, we not only conserve resources, we produce them. Well-managed organizational conflict could prove to be your number one wellspring of resource generation and one of your most powerful management tools.

2.

TAKING CHARGE OF
ORGANIZATIONAL CONFLICT

2. THE SOURCES OF CONFLICT

While the primary ingredients in any conflict are the individuals involved, conflicts tend to spring from the same litany of sources for all people, and virtually every conflict begins with someone or something violating an individual's "comfort zone."

Each of us defines our "comfort zone" by erecting limits on what we perceive to be acceptable, allowable, "safe" experiences and behaviors. Any event that intrudes, threatens or assaults our comfort zone, or requires us to move beyond the limits of our comfort zone, produces conflict. Our first awareness of conflict comes from the feelings that are produced when the comfort zone is violated.

Feelings of dissatisfaction comprise a related *internal* source of conflict. When we feel dissatisfied (disappointed) or unsatisfied (unfulfilled), we experience varying levels of discomfort, which in turn produce or augment conflict.

Since all of us have a natural preference for feeling comfortable, we tend to respond to discomfort in ways that we believe will restore comfort. In biology, this phenomenon is referred to as *homeostasis* — the organism returning to a state of equilibrium.

> Homeostasis:
>
> A state of physiological equilibrium produced by a balance of functions and chemical composition

Certain categories of conflict are common. By exploring some of these categories, we can start to recognize the seeds of conflict even before they sprout, and we can consciously choose appropriate responses early, while the conflict is still small. Here are some of the more common comfort-zone issues that lead to conflict:

Basic Emotional Needs

Collectively, these are our "hot buttons." Everyone has them. The three most significant in terms of conflict are the need to be valued or loved, the need to be in control, and the need to like ourselves or enjoy a sense of self-worth.

The Need to be Valued or Loved has to do with how we imagine others perceive us. If for any reason we believe that our value in the eyes of others is being (or going to be) compromised, we immediately become uncomfortable, experiencing internal conflict related to restoring the perception we want others to have of us. For example, when an employee is corrected or reprimanded by a supervisor in front of a coworker, the employee is likely to experience extreme discomfort concerning the probability that his or her image has been diminished in the eyes of this peer. The relative importance of the other person's perception of the employee is the gauge that determines the degree of discomfort and conflict experienced. The greater our desire for a person's love and approval, the greater the discomfort and conflict when the flow of love and approval is reduced or interrupted.

The Need to be in Control means the need to feel like we are in control of ourselves and our destiny — that we have options, and that we are free and able to make choices. Whenever we sense that we are, or are about to be, out of control, we experience discomfort proportional to the extent of the loss. Severe discomfort and, consequently, intense conflict can result. When, for example, an entire department is suddenly required to align its production schedule with new quotas and procedures mandated by upper management, the members of the department may feel as though the reins of control have been snatched from their hands.

When loss of control is a source of conflict, it always draws in other people. Control in this context does not mean control of others, although one of the first things people often do to restore a sense of self-control is attempt to control others. This remedy may give the illusion of working, but usually doesn't.

The Need to Like Ourselves and Have a Sense of Self-Worth is related to the level of our self-esteem. Anything that causes us to feel inadequate, or incapable of achieving an expectation, threatens this important sense of well-being. Interestingly, having the ability to manage the conflicts and confrontations in our lives greatly contributes to our ability to like and think well of ourselves.

TRY THIS!

Here's a way for you to get to know more about yourself and what your "Hot Buttons" actually are —

For two weeks keep a journal, recording the times you feel angry. Each time you make an entry, note which of your "hot buttons" has been pushed. After two weeks, you will have a very good picture of your vulnerability to anger.

Personal Values and Beliefs

As we grow, each of us develops a set of values and beliefs that shape all of our behavior. Whenever we perceive an event or condition to be incongruous with one of these beliefs or values, we are pulled out of our comfort zone and experience conflict. When, for example, a manager is required by Human Resources (under pressure from top management) to take a severe no tolerance position with respect to jokes, remarks and casual conversation with sexual overtones, the manager may experience conflict between his or her own values and those imposed by a higher (but somewhat remote) authority. The stronger the belief or the more important the value, the greater the discomfort and attendant conflict. Because we are so diverse with respect to our beliefs and values, it is impossible for two people, let alone groups of people, to see eye to eye on everything.

Ideas, Opinions, and Issues

We all have ideas about things. As an idea develops, it can rather quickly turn into an opinion. Sometimes we express opinions by saying things like, "The way I see it ..." or "I think ..." Our opinions are formed from the raw materials of our belief systems. As an idea takes shape, it often becomes an opinion based on what we believe.

We don't form our opinions by accident. Almost all opinions are formed in relation to an existing issue, an issue being any topic around which there are already at least two different opinions. An issue can be very simple or very complex. For example, when two people each want to watch a different television program, we have one issue and two opinions. But when politicians debate health care reform, we have one main issue, thousands of sub-issues, and tens of thousands of opinions.

Opinions and issues are a good place to look to find conflicts. We would do well to remember when expressing opinions that other people are likely to have different or *opposing* opinions. The existence of opposing opinions can and often does produce conflict, the seriousness of which is determined by the strength of and emotional attachment to those opinions.

Some issues don't involve other people. For example, let's say that you are facing a major deadline on a project, and you have to make a decision between working or going with friends to the theatre. Behind this simple decision lie two conflicting opinions, each based on entirely reasonable beliefs. On the one hand, you hold the opinion that refusing to go with friends may jeopardize friendships and deny you an enjoyable evening. Supporting this belief is the rationale that, even if you go to the theatre, you may still be able to devote a few late hours to your project. Finally, you believe that going out with friends is a healthy thing to do.

On the other hand, you think that your friends will probably understand and respect a decision to stay home and work. Furthermore, you know that taking care of the task will bolster your self-image. Finally, you believe that if you go to the theatre you'll put so much energy into dreading the work ahead and worrying about your deadline that you won't enjoy yourself anyway.

You have two conflicting opinions based on two sets of beliefs. As long as it continues unresolved, the conflict itself steals energy from both alternatives!

Facts and Information

How many times have you heard or seen facts and information that seem contradictory? Our perceptions have a lot to do with this. Since each of us sees and interprets things somewhat uniquely, our perception of "the facts" may be different from the perceptions of other people. Very often, "facts" are really opinions. Is it a fact that the new incentive program is discriminatory and overly expensive, or is it the opinion of a small but vocal minority? Sometimes, facts are not complete and information is left out. What does the hard data say and how and by whom is that data being interpreted? Whenever we deal with facts and information we need to be aware that what appears a certain way to us doesn't necessarily look that way to others.

Processes and Methods

Seldom is there just one way of doing something. Since processes and methods affect outcomes, people often become contentious defending them. Even something as simple as selecting the route to take in traveling from one place to another can produce conflict because the route (method) affects the time spent getting there, among other things. The more importance ascribed to the outcome, or the more commitment given a particular process or method, the greater the intensity of discomfort and conflict.

Similarities and Differences

Diversity can also breed conflict. People are different by virtue of their belief systems, human traits, and conditioned responses; in other words, by who they are. And they differ in many other ways, too. Most people acknowledge this fact but fail to take it into account when confrontations arise. Developing an awareness of the ways we differ is important if we are to move toward higher levels of inclusion and accommodation.

In truth, we are more alike than different.

TRY THIS!

1. Get a group of people together, and ask them to name all the ways they differ from one another. The answers come quickly, and include personality, preferences, skills, intelligence, traditions, culture, race, etc. In moments, you'll have a long list of differences.

2. Next, ask them to name all the ways they are *exactly* the same. This list will be slow in forming. Usually someone will say that everyone present is a human being. Someone else may suggest that everyone has the same basic needs or the same anatomy. This is where the second list generally stops.

At first glance, these two lists support the notion that people are different from one another, but pursue the question farther:

Now ask the group to think about the list of differences, and find a way to turn those differences into *exact* likenesses. Try it. Think about everyone having a *different* personality. Now put aside the "different" for a moment, and consider the fact that everyone *has* a personality, just as everyone has preferences, skills, intelligence, traditions, culture, race, etc. When you teach people to think about differences this way, they start to see how truly alike they are.

By failing to see how much alike we are, we are planting seeds of conflict. Focusing only on the belief that we are different from one another actually produces conflict.

Turf

We begin to learn about possessions and territory from our earliest experiences. Collectively, possessions and territory comprise our "turf." Many cultures place a high premium on "getting" as a measure of success. A T-shirt reads, "He who dies with the most toys wins." A good question to ask is: "...wins what?"

Holding this belief, we move through life measuring our success by how much we obtain. We become acutely aware of intrusions upon and threats to our turf. When we lose something, we feel a discomfort akin to failure. If we lose enough, we may come to see *ourselves* as failures — a serious and destructive conclusion. It is very difficult to change an individual's identification with material possessions, but it is not so difficult to develop the skills necessary to constructively deal with conflicts involving turf.

People who work together benefit by recognizing that the ultimate value of their turf, like their diversity, lies in its ability to contribute to a larger system.

> It is vital that as people work together, they recognize that the real value of their turf ultimately lies in its ability to contribute to a larger system.

Conflicts that arise from issues of turf can be small or global. When a neighbor's dog finds a handy place in the middle of our front yard to discharge a bodily function, we experience a small intrusion onto our turf. The events of September 11th were intrusions onto our national turf that went on to engage global involvment. Similarly, when we read of the rapid destruction of the rainforest, we are seeing a large intrusion onto our global turf. It has a much different look, but varies only in appearance. So it is with turf issues in organizations. In an organization, the turf issues are different, but no less important.

Taking Charge of Organizational Conflict proposes that each of us use all of our resources, including our turf, to contribute to the success of the organization and, in the process, the success of those around us.

Limited Resources

Organizations never seem to have enough of everything for everyone. Because they are limited, resources must be allocated, and the process of determining who gets what can put the wheels of conflict in high gear. As we compete for resources, we are automatically cast into win-lose situations that often hinge on politics rather than equity or fairness and always boil down to conflict.

Only when individuals see themselves in a picture of organizational success, can they subordinate personal concerns to organizational good.

Although conflicts arising from issues of limited resources may be expressed overtly, they are more often reflected in low morale, or reduced productivity justified as the inevitable result of insufficient resources.

> All change produces conflict, and every conflict produces change.
>
> The quality of change is determined by the skill with which conflict is managed and resolved.

Change

Change is a constant. Every organization undergoes continuous change, and every individual deals with change at both personal and professional levels. The introduction of any change requires that we expand our comfort zone to accommodate the change, or rail against it in a state of conflict until we either surrender to the change or it goes away.

Wherever we see a failed effort to bring about change, we always see a case of poorly managed conflict. Therefore, each of us must be aware that all change produces conflict and the extent to which we are able to take charge of that conflict will determine the success we have with change. Examples of this are all around us. All we have to do is think of an instance when we tried to change a habit or loose weight. If it was a struggle, it was conflict.

One Right Answer

This is the most potent source of conflict. Considering how much people differ, the potential for conflict between individuals is easy to see. Add to the differences just one ingredient and conflict is virtually *guaranteed*. This ingredient is simply the need to be right. The need to be right is an integral part of our survival mechanisms and is at the root of virtually every interpersonal conflict. If you and I are different, and we both believe that only one of us is right, that automatically makes one of us wrong, and we have created a conflict over which of us holds title to the truth.

Buckminster Fuller estimated that by about 10,000 BC major inventions were occurring every couple of hundred years or so. By the beginning of the Christian era, they may have been happening every fifty years. By about 1700, the time period was reduced to thirty years. In our current period, major inventions are taking place virtually monthly.

The message I want to emphasize is that for the first time ever the period of doubling of all human activity has been reduced to less than a human generation. We humans just aren't accustomed to that rate of change. The engine is winding up, and up, and up, getting faster and faster. How long can we endure this rate of change?

We all know that this pace has become so fast and so furious that our institutions are breaking down. Nothing seems to be working. We're getting ahead of ourselves. And the question is, what in the world are we going to do about it?

Comments by Edgar Mitchell,
Apollo Astronaut

Where did our need to be right come from? In a very real sense it is one of our basic human needs. Typically we have a need to be right rather than wrong. This is further reinforced as we grow up through our experiences in the home and in broader society. It happenened in school as well. Classrooms and teachers bombarded us with the notion that there was only one right answer. Those who knew the answer were rewarded with attention, approval, and good grades, and those who didn't know the answer experienced criticism, rejection, and bad grades. Many years later, we still defend to the wall our right to be right!

Learning to understand, respect, and appreciate similarities and differences is one key to resolving conflicts and is essential if we are to build on diversity and realize inclusion and interdependence. From the moment we accept the fallacious notion that there is only one right answer, we close our minds to the ideas of other people, and limit ourselves to only one point of view. By recognizing that other answers have validity and value, we can expand our comfort zone and open ourselves to new information and personal growth.

These are a few of the primary sources of conflict. Although many other sources undoubtedly exist, the most important thing to understand is that all conflicts grow from having someone or something violate our individual comfort zone.

Because conflict is a naturally occurring process and because of the enormous diversity that surrounds us, it is not possible to eliminate conflict, nor is it possible to avoid it. What is possible is to achieve a reduction in the numbers of conflicts and their debilitating consequences.

Resolving a conflict doesn't necessarily eliminate the source of the conflict. In all likelihood, people will continue to hold divergent positions and opinions. However, when a conflict is well managed, it is possible for individuals to maintain their beliefs and at the same time understand, accommodate, and accept the beliefs and behaviors of others.

3.

TAKING CHARGE OF
ORGANIZATIONAL CONFLICT

3. DYNAMICS OF CONFLICT

In preparing to deal more effectively with conflict, each of us needs to know three important things: First, conflict is a natural part of being alive — a natural process in which we all engage. Second, because conflict is a natural process, it is not realistic to think we are going to be able to avoid it. Finally, since we are going to be in conflict from time to time, we need to be aware of some of the ways it is likely to affect us.

Whether it involves others, conflict affects us personally. It is at this level that the ability to manage conflict well has its greatest potential. To the extent that conflict absorbs our thinking and our time, it distracts us from the important things we have to do and want to do. It can drain energy, produce distress, and negatively color our decisions and influence our relations with others. When we are able to effectively take control of conflict at the personal level, we can turn these results around, not only maintaining ground, but producing higher levels of individual effectiveness, productivity and creativity not to mention being happier and more satisfied.

Conflict in an organization affects not only those who are directly involved, it also impacts those who are indirectly involved — the "innocent bystanders." Directly or indirectly, everyone connected with a conflict is affected at a personal level.

The quality of conflict management at the personal level has a direct relationship to the quality of conflict management organizationally. Good conflict management begins with the individuals involved. If the disputants are able to take charge of and manage themselves in the conflict situation, the outcome is always positive. This holds true in both interpersonal (external) conflicts (those involving others) and internal conflicts where the dispute may be with thoughts, ideas, or things. However, in most organizations, not enough people possess the awareness or the skills to do this. It is neither realistic nor necessary to expect every member of an organization to be a skilled peacemaker. An organization should strive, instead, to prepare a critical mass of people to take charge of personal and organizational conflicts when they arise.

Poorly managed organizational conflict will always lead to negative, and largely unnecessary, outcomes.

Every conflict produces a result or consequence. If we think of conflict as a process, we see that it invariably leads to a conclusion. Some conflicts are resolved very quickly, others may take a lifetime to resolve, but one way or another they all come to an end.

All conflicts produce change as a consequence. Since conflict is dynamic, change starts taking place the minute a conflict begins and doesn't end until it is resolved. For better or worse, when conflict begins, everything and everybody associated with it begins to change. The quality of the change produced by conflict is determined by the skill with which the conflict is managed and resolved.

By first considering some general notions about unmanaged internal and external conflict, and then exploring the concept of "win-lose" in conflict situations, we can make some important connections to the realities of organizational conflict as it relates to customers (those for whom we do our work), suppliers (those who provide work that supports us), and the impact of conflict on resources. Our aim is to learn how the evolution of conflict can be controlled, then managed, and then turned to our advantage.

UNMANAGED CONFLICT EQUALS DESTRUCTIVE CONSEQUENCES

Organizations are rife with opportunities for conflict. All the individuals who are a part of an organization, or who have any interest or involvement with it, bring to the organization the accumulation of everything they've learned — all of their habits and all the beliefs they've developed about themselves, other people, and their world. Such diversity makes conflict inevitable. And because the conflict-resolution skills of most people are poorly developed, the outcomes of conflict are frequently negative — at times even destructive.

Let's look at what we're likely to experience as a result of poorly managed conflict, both intrapersonal and interpersonal:

Intrapersonal conflict is the most difficult form of conflict to deal with, because one of the unfortunate habits most of us have developed is a lack of sufficient trust in other people. If we don't feel safe involving those around us who can help, a conflict may fester and go unnoticed by everyone who might be of assistance. When this happens, we experience a variety of consequences — all negative. First, because we are experiencing distress, not only are we distracted from our work, the neuro-mechanisms required for us to learn or be effective contributors are rendered inoperable. In this condition, both our productivity and potential are compromised.

As we struggle with intrapersonal conflict, a sense of inadequacy starts to develop. We convince ourselves that we are out of control, and perhaps not even capable of resolving the conflict. Looking about, we perceive that others are successfully coping with everything in their lives. Little-by-little, self-esteem is eroded, and we develop a sense of vulnerability. We may become isolated and lash out at those who offer assistance, interpreting their efforts as intrusions. Serious personal, social, and performance consequences may result, reinforcing past experiences and creating a cycle that can eventually destroy any chance of a positive work-related experience.

> Internal conflict doesn't just affect the person directly involved — it affects everyone who is involved with that person.

This isn't a very happy picture and may seem extreme, but it is happening everywhere. It is happening in your organization, and, if you think about it, you probably know someone who is caught in this cycle right now.

But doesn't intrapersonal conflict only affect the person experiencing the conflict? No. Others depend on us to be productive. Our inability to perform can have an adverse effect on them, may require additional time and attention from our supervisor, and may be felt by others with whom we interact as customers or suppliers.

FROM DISAGREEMENT TO CRISIS

The results of interpersonal conflict are similar to those of intrapersonal conflict, but are usually broader because more people are involved.

Interpersonal conflict usually begins with a disagreement. At this point, good conflict-resolution skills can have an immediate effect. More often than not, however, complications multiply and feelings escalate to the point where intervention may be required. Disruptions caused by conflict spell disastrous consequences for any organization. Time spent restoring peace is lost forever. Relationships and egos may be damaged, and the resulting tension inhibits productivity.

The most terrible consequence of interpersonal conflict is violence. When people do not have the skills to resolve conflicts, they automatically resort to whatever methods they've learned, often choosing aggression or complete withdrawal. At opposite ends of the response spectrum, aggression and withdrawal can be equally destructive. Aggression at its worst generates violent acts toward others; withdrawal and passivity at their worst generate violent acts toward the self. If you doubt that this scenario is possible just listen to the news. When we hear about violent acts in the workplace, we often think of the perpetrators as strange or evil people. They are not. For the most part they are just average people who lost control of situations that could have been managed.

> The consequences of an unmanaged or poorly managed conflict are disproportionately larger than the conflict itself

A workable rule of thumb holds that the consequences of an unmanaged or poorly managed conflict are disproportionately larger than the conflict itself. We should keep this rule in mind when we are tempted to dismiss a conflict because we don't think it requires our attention. Nowhere in life is the adage "an ounce of prevention is worth a pound of cure" more applicable than in the realm of conflict.

TRY THIS!

Regardless of the group size, ask people to take a moment and think back to a time when they experienced, directly or indirectly: A Time Something Small Developed Into Something Big.

Elaborate: Suggest that the occasion could have been either personal or professional. They could have been involved in the incident, or just an observer. In either case, what started out as a minor incident quickly turned into something serious, involving children or adults, individuals or groups, or even organizations. Tell participants to think of an example, recall it in detail, and be prepared to share those details with the rest of the group.

Give your audience about sixty seconds to think of a conflict situation that fits this description and then ask volunteers to describe the incident to the group.

When four or five participants have shared, ask the group the following questions to generate a discussion:

— *As you think back to the situation, what things could have been done to prevent the conflict from escalating?*

— *In what ways can having greater skill in managing conflicts help us to contain small conflicts and keep them from becoming more serious?*

WIN-LOSE AND LOSE-LOSE

Over the years, we've heard a lot about win-win, win-lose, and lose-lose. Our culture consistently places the highest value on winning, often at any cost. Sporting events of all kinds glorify winning and denigrate losing ("the agony of defeat"). We tend to carry this attitude over to the conflict arena, which is considerably more complicated. The only real choices in conflict are win-win and lose-lose. Win-lose is just another form of lose-lose. Sometimes we don't have the option to produce a win-win, but in almost every case we can reduce the degree of loss suffered by carefully and thought-fully engineering a lose-lose that minimizes negative consequences. This is sometimes referred to as "cutting our losses."

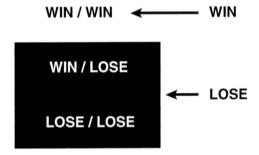

In the final analysis, no one wins in an organizational conflict unless everyone wins. Any member of an organization who perceives him- or herself as a loser can be expected to produce losses for the organization as well, whether those losses be in the form of reduced morale, damaged communication, lowered productivity, faction-building, or some other consequence. However, even in losing we can produce learning and growth as mitigating by-products. I believe that we can adopt a win-win spirit and can learn to effectively manage and resolve conflicts, and that the attitudes and skills required are transferable to every part of our lives for as long as we live.

WELL-MANAGED CONFLICT EQUALS POSITIVE CHANGE AND PERSONAL GROWTH

We need to be able to recognize when we're experiencing a conflict and to know whether the conflict is internal (intrapersonal) or external (interpersonal) in nature. With this awareness, we can begin to identify resources to help resolve the conflict, and develop the skill and trust necessary to reach out to those resources.

One of the things that characterizes high-performing organizations is a well-developed willingness and ability among workers to collaborate in resolving conflict. Individuals are able to clearly define the problems that underlie conflicts, and select or develop strategies for bringing about their resolution. People engage in conflict with conscious awareness that they are involved in a process, and every time they join to resolve a conflict, they reinforce their skills and enhance their ability to constructively handle future conflict well. This promotes significant personal growth; people see themselves as capable of dealing effectively with conflict and interacting positively with others in the process. Self-esteem is enhanced, the need to belong is satisfied, and employees experience a kind of bonding that produces unity and cohesiveness. The work place is then perceived as generative and the organization is seen as something people want to be a part of.

> Far beyond the positive social consequences of effectively taking charge of organizational conflict are the measurable increases in individual and group effectiveness and productivity.

All of these positive consequences occur when conflicts are well managed and skillfully resolved. In addition, organizations experience greater intergroup harmony as people whose differences have caused them to polarize into political, issue-centered, ethnic, intellectual, or social factions begin to appreciate and value each other's similarities and differences.

More importantly, the organization benefits from increased individual and group effectiveness and higher levels of productivity.

THE WIN-WIN OUTCOME

The ultimate organizational result is a win-win climate in which all those who participate in a conflict and all those who are affected by it realize positive outcomes.

This scenario sounds so nice that it's hard to imagine anyone not wanting to learn and exercise the necessary skills and abilities; still, two constraining factors must be addressed: To effectively develop the skills related to managing conflict, an active effort at organizational or staff development must be undertaken. Next, the program must be sustained and consistently applied in order for change to take place. Change takes time, but more importantly, it takes commitment. A degree of commitment sufficient to get the program started and keep it going until it becomes an integral, self-sustaining part of the organization. Research and practical experience have demonstrated over and over again that wherever conflict resolution programs have been undertaken and sustained over periods of a year or more, significant results have been achieved.

> You can't win arguments, but you can win agreement.

For any program of organizational conflict management to be effective the following two conditions must be met:

1. An active effort at professional and staff development must be undertaken.

2. The program, once implemented, must be sustained and consistently applied.

The positive and negative consequences of conflict are opposite sides of the same coin. Moving from one side to the other is not accomplished by flipping the coin, but by turning it over slowly. This needn't be difficult, but it does take time. As you increase your understanding and appreciation of conflict, you'll see that conflict has great potential.

CONNECTING CONFLICT TO PRODUCTIVITY

Beyond the general implications of conflict in organizations, we can begin to look at specific areas where conflict influences productivity. Since everything begins with the individual, the connection between a person's ability to deal with conflict and his or her self-esteem is a link that cannot be overlooked.

The Self-Esteem Connection

In spite of all the scathing editorials and cynical cartoons afforded the "self-esteem movement," recognition of the importance of self-esteem is more widespread today than ever before. In its final report, the California Task Force to Promote Self-esteem and Personal and Social Responsibility had this to say about improving levels of self-esteem for all of us:

"The building blocks of self-esteem are skills. The more skillful a person, the more likely that he or she will be able to cope in life situations. By fostering skills of personal and social responsibility, [people] increase their behavioral options. Having a number of behavioral options makes it easier to make ethical choices and develop skills to function effectively."

Of these social skills, the ability to manage confrontations and conflict ranks near the top. Years ago, it became apparent that training efforts directed at human resource development were paying big dividends in productivity. Direct links were made between individual and organizational effectiveness and the quality and quantity of training workers received.

Key Skills and Attributes

Listening

Oral Communications

Trusting

Responsiblity

Integrity

Initiative

Conflict Management

Decision Making

Time Managment

Goal Setting

Stress Management

It was determined that training directed solely at job-related tasks (technical training), when taken by itself, was far less effective in improving performance than was technical training augmented by training in the skills and attributes associated with improving interpersonal relations. Research from the Carnegie Foundation tells us that as much as 85 percent of job success is due to well-developed interpersonal skills while only about 15 percent results from technical skills. The research goes on to make the same connection to performance-related job loss.

When workers felt more competent, they became more effective and in turn more productive. Later on, it was discovered that when workers felt more competent and produced at higher levels, they felt better about themselves and their organizations.

Today, as we look at the research connected with self-esteem, it becomes apparent that when we assist people to become more competent, not just at what they do but in their relations with co-workers, self-esteem goes up right along with productivity. This heightened self-esteem is more the result of increased ability to perform than it is the cause of increased performance.

> Self esteem is the result of feeling more able to do something than it is the cause of doing something better.

Organizations, too, have self-esteem. Organizational self-esteem is reflective of the level of esteem in which individuals hold the organization and themselves within the context of the organization. The model on the following page illustrates this connection for individuals, groups and organizations.

Looking at the model, notice the term acknowledging. Remember that it is not enough to have a skill. People need to feel that they possess a skill to the extent that they are able to perform at high levels. This "feeling able" is the acknowledgment to which the model refers.

DEVELOPING SELF-ESTEEM

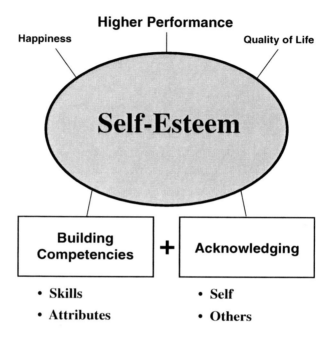

When individuals engage in the process of conflict (and they surely do), the effect of conflict on individual and organizational self-esteem is determined by the level of competence they bring to its management and resolution.

When organizations help employees productively manage conflict, they increase levels of self-esteem for both individuals and the organization while at the same time increasing effectiveness and productivity.

Two measures of organizational self-esteem are workplace satisfaction and job satisfaction. If yours is an organization that causes people to wish they were elsewhere, it is a place

An interesting side note to the discussion of self esteem is that it is fluid. That is, it tends to be situational. A person's self esteem can vary widely from situation to situation. As we move through a day, we can find ourselves in many different environments each of which presents differing situations. If these are conflict situations, and we are prepared to deal with them effectively, our self esteem not only remains high, as a result, it goes higher with each success. Moreover, when we are faced with a situation where things go poorly, we have built up the resilience to look at the result objectively and draw from it whatever lessons it offers.

where people find their self-esteem threatened. In this regard, it is an organization with low self-esteem. On the other hand, if employees take pride in the organization and derive positive feelings from their association with it, organizational self-esteem is already relatively high.

TRY THIS!

Group Work

Note: Before beginning Group Work activities, review the "Group Work Guidelines" beginning on Page 189

If you want a window into how people feel about being in your organization, get one or more groups together (no more than six or eight people in a group). Using the Group Work Guidelines, ask each person to share with the group on the topic, "One of My Favorite Places."

Here's an idea for elaborating —

This place doesn't need to be your all-time favorite . . . just a place you like to be. It could be a simple place or it could be exotic. Maybe it's a place you enjoy alone or one you enjoy with friends or family. It can be a place you frequent or one to which you have only been once. Tell us about the place and why it's a favorite. Describe how you feel when you are there, when you tell others about it, or when you just recall it. Take moment to think it over. The topic is, "One of My Favorite Places."

When everyone who wishes to share has done so, ask this question:

— *What did the things we shared seem to have in common?*

After a little discussion, ask these questions:

— *Is where you work one of your favorite places? Why or why not?*

After the small groups have finished their discussions, convene the entire group for further discussion. Ask individuals to describe what they discovered in their sharing groups. You'll learn a lot about people and how your organization affects their self-esteem. You'll also have some idea of your organization's level of self-esteem.

The Quality Connection

Every organization or industry has a vocabulary to describe its customers — the people, groups or organizations to whom it provides products or services.

No matter what an organization may think, it is the customer to whom it is ultimately accountable. Since an organization is nothing more than its people, each person in an

> Your customers are any persons or groups who are influenced by or who influence the organization or its people.

organization is also ultimately accountable to the customer. Unfortunately, most people in organizations, aren't yet seeing the accountability picture this way.

In an age when great emphasis is being placed on "quality management," this accountability gap is proving to be the organization's Achilles' Heel. Not only don't people feel a high level of commitment to the customer, most people don't even know who the customer is. In retail organizations, for instance, purchasers of merchandise are certainly customers, but so are all the people and groups that are influenced by, or who influence, the organization and its employees. In the current vernacular, these people are usually referred to as stakeholders or publics. Whatever we call them, they're not just the folks at the cash register.

Do a mental inventory. Count every person inside and outside your organization who does something that contributes to or inhibits the work you do. For better or worse, you are their customer and they are your suppliers. Now think about all the people *your* work helps or hinders. They are your customers and you are *their* supplier. The truth is that if people associated with an organization are not both suppliers and customers, they don't belong in that organization!

TRY THIS!

To better understand the concept of "customers," remind your group that customers are any persons or groups who are influenced by, or who influence, the organization or its people; then ask members of your audience to name their customers. As ideas are shared, use a chalkboard or chart pad to record them. Leave room on the right so that you can come back after the list is complete and identify each customer as either internal (within the organization) or external (clients, consumers, etc.). *Tip — Allocate plenty of room for recording and working with this information.*

When complete, post the list. On a new sheet of paper, draw a large circle leaving room outside the circle to record data. Now create a web of your organization and its community cohorts showing how each is linked in customer-supplier relationships. Put internal customers/suppliers (integral parts of the organization) inside the circle. Place external customers/suppliers outside the circle.

When all the links are made, ask the group where in the web they think conflicts are likely to develop.

As an organization engages in any quality management process, strategy, or other endeavor, the greatest opportunities and the biggest stumbling blocks are usually found in the intricacies of all these emerging relationships. Changes of the magnitude produced by such transitions always produce conflict. Any effort at changing the culture of an organization is absolutely doomed if people are not prepared to deal effectively with conflict. The reason for this is simple. A shift toward higher quality (or any other form of organizational transformation) will produce high levels of conflict as people try to sort out emerging roles, responsibilities and relationships, and as they engage in the very human response of resisting change. If not dealt with productively, the resulting conflict is likely to slow the effort to a snail's pace, if not completely derail it.

Consider this: Creativity, innovation, and growth all produce conflict. Remembering that conflict is a process, those organizations that are creative, innovative, and growing are organizations that are taking charge of conflict and turning it to a productive process. This doesn't mean they are undisciplined or unstructured. They simply know what to do and do it when it comes to conflict. Any organization that wants to be seen this way had better think about this fact.

Even if your organization is not pursuing any sort of transformation, it still has all of the dynamic human interactions just described. Organizations are about people interacting with people, and those interactions produce conflict.

Organizations that have not prepared people to do well in conflict situations experience unpleasant consequences, often perceiving them as unavoidable. Such organizations may conclude that the only way to restore peace is to stop doing the things that produced the conflict. If efforts at positive change produced the conflict, ineffective organizations are apt to abandon those efforts in favor of maintaining what appears to be the more peaceful status quo. In this regard, the ability to take charge of conflict is directly related to organizational growth and success.

Keep in mind that it's easy to confuse the process of conflict with the outcomes of poorly managed conflict. Organizations that are thriving generally have as much or more conflict than organizations that are struggling or standing still. Because they manage the process better, they enjoy the paradox of peaceful and productive conflict.

The Resource Connection

It may seem strange connecting resource management and conflict, but the two are inseparably connected and together can impinge upon the success of any organization.

All organizations rely on finite resources to accomplish their undertakings. Every activity pursued by an individual or organization to some extent consumes resources. Resources are either hard (*e.g.*, materials, space, money,) or soft (*e.g.*, time, energy or morale). Every activity competes for these limited resources, so they are best used to generate maximum positive results.

Since conflict is not an activity that most organizations consider primary, and is usually thought of as counterproductive, organizations are surprised to see how many resources conflict ultimately consumes.

TRY THIS!

Group Work (See Page 189)

To help people make a personal connection between resources and conflict, use the topic, "Something That Is Distracting Me From Being as Productive as I Can Be."

Here's an idea for elaborating —

Think about the things that you would like to be doing in terms of fulfilling your responsibilities. Then consider all of the things that seem to distract you from these tasks and the ways these distractions impede your performance. Distractions can be little things that other people do that bother you, they can be policies or procedures that stand in your way, or they can be personal concerns. Take time to consider all the things, personal and professional, internal and external, that get in your way. Take a few moments and then we will talk about, "Something That Is Distracting Me From Being as Productive as I Can Be."

After everyone has had a chance to share, facilitate a discussion with the following question:

— In what ways are our distractions connected to conflict? (They produce or contribute to conflict.)

Now reconvene the total group and ask people to name some of the distractions they shared in their small groups. List these, leaving about a four-inch margin on the right side for use in an upcoming activity (page 59).

To drive home your point, brainstorm a list of the different kinds of resources that are consumed when people are distracted from important tasks. Record this list on the board or on chart paper. Then ask participants to think about the cumulative impact of these distractions and what dealing with them more productively might mean to the organization and to them personally.

All organizations, big and small, engage in conflict and in so doing consume resources. The question then is not whether an organization is going to experience conflict, but to what extent and with what results. War offers a global example. Organized societies very often find themselves in disputes (conflicts) that, because they are poorly managed, deteriorate into wars or armed conflicts. These conflicts can be internal (civil wars) or external (World Wars I and II, etc.).

It is not difficult to see that wars require enormous quantities of both hard and soft resources. Unlike most organizational conflicts, however, wars always consume the priceless resource of human lives.

According to our definition of conflict as a process, war is the outcome of a poorly-managed conflict. Historically, it may be argued that our years of conflict with the former Soviet Union, referred to as the "cold war," represented a much better-managed conflict than the nuclear holocaust that might have resulted had the conflict been handled with less skill. It is useful also to consider that though enormous resources were appropriated in preparing for war, the productive technological by-products of this preparation were enormous.

> To some degree every conflict absorbs both hard and soft resources. The manner in which these resources are used determines the quality of the outcomes generated by the conflict.

These global examples are analogous to what organizations experience when they are confronted with conflict. To some degree, every conflict absorbs both hard and soft resources. The manner in which these resources are used determines the quality of the outcomes generated by the conflict.

Though most organizations don't experience results akin to war, the results can be very damaging. On the other hand, when well managed, conflicts have the potential to produce growth and expand creativity.

Since every organization experiences conflict, every conflict consumes resources, and conflict is just as likely to produce positive as negative results, being able to effectively take charge of the conflicts that naturally occur in an organization presents a significant opportunity that most organizations are not taking full advantage of.

This opportunity has two dimensions. The first has to do with simply reducing the numbers and severity of conflicts that arise. Since to varying degrees, all organizations devote resources to conflict, it stands to reason that fewer resources needlessly wasted on conflict mean more resources for the primary concerns of the organization. Organizations waste resources on conflict when they fail to prepare people to deal with it effectively. The following graph gives a picture of just what is meant by redirecting resources by better managing conflict:

BETTER CONFLICT MANAGEMENT EQUALS RESOURCE CONSERVATION

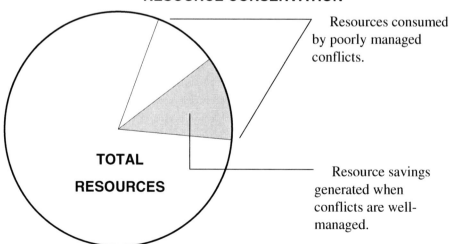

Resources consumed by poorly managed conflicts.

TOTAL RESOURCES

Resource savings generated when conflicts are well-managed.

Conflicts will still arise, but well-managed conflicts consume fewer resources. Preparing an organization to deal effectively with conflict literally pays off in resources freed up to support more productive activities. In this way, better management of conflict can be thought of as resource conservation.

The second dimension builds on the first and has to do with using conflict management to not only maintain or reestablish peace and harmony in the organization, but to promote positive outcomes from those conflict situations that do arise.

The following chart contrasts the results that are likely to flow from both poorly- and well-managed conflicts:

CONSEQUENCES OF PERSONAL AND PROFESSIONAL CONFLICT

Poorly or Unmanaged Conflict (Negative Results)	Well-Managed Conflict (Positive Results)
Slows learning and growth	Promotes learning and growth
Reduces productivity and effectiveness	Enhances productivity and effectiveness
Damages relationships	Strengthens relationships
Discourages cooperation	Stimulates and reinforces cooperation
Destroys trust	Builds trust and dialogue
Stifles creativity and innovation	Generates creativity and innovation
Creates defensiveness	Promotes safety and interdependence
Produces hidden agendas	Generates openness
Wastes, time money and human resources	Increases efficiency
Focuses on blaming and fault-finding	Produces sense of responsibility
Creates enemies and hard feelings	Strengthens relationships
Produces stress and drains energy	Redirects energy to productive outcome
Generates hostility and violence	Promotes peace and harmony

The positive consequences go far beyond just maintaining peace and harmony. Every conflict holds within it the potential to produce growth and to enhance the quality, effectiveness and productivity of individual employees and, in turn, the organization. The following chart graphically portrays this potential:

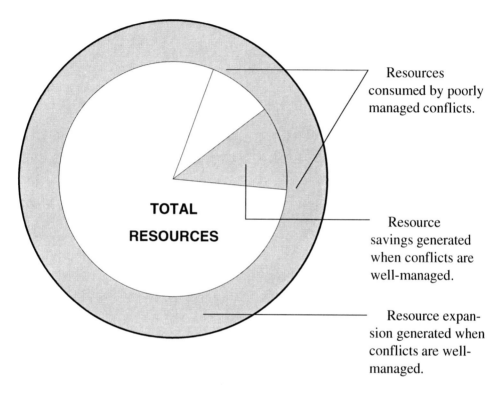

Resources consumed by poorly managed conflicts.

Resource savings generated when conflicts are well-managed.

Resource expansion generated when conflicts are well-managed.

These results are significant! This potential for creativity should cause every organization to invest substantially in conflict management.

> Every conflict has creative potential. Managing them well harnesses this potential

Virtually all creativity flows from conflict. When we manage conflicts well, the resources that are consumed as part of the process of conflict resolution frequently contribute to creative, innovative and productive outcomes.

Most of what we see today as the creative output of organizational effort is in some way related to conflict. The degree to which this is true for any single organization depends upon the quality of conflict management the organization is capable of producing.

> It is the potential conflict management has of conserving resources and promoting creativity that makes taking charge of organizational conflict an essential ingredient in organizations that hope to maximize productivity and achieve excellence.

Thus, we have moved beyond the conservation of resources to define conflict as a truly generative process. The potential of conflict management to conserve resources and promote creativity makes taking charge of organizational conflict an essential activity in organizations that hope to maximize productivity and achieve excellence.

The Organization Connection

Although prevailing thought may favor driving conflict out of organizations, this is an exercise in futility that consumes more resources and tends to produce more conflict. The best approach is to acknowledge that conflict is here to stay and to go about finding effective ways of dealing with it.

Neutralizing conflict is squandering a great opportunity. Failing to harness the creative potential of conflict is a mistake most organizations make. Another is to underestimate the residual effects of conflict, such as its influence on interpersonal and organizational trust.

> Trust is fragile and conflict always has an influence. It is important to think of trust as an asset. When we possess it either as individuals or organizations we are richer.

Most successful organizational strategies rely heavily on developing and maintaining high levels of trust, and few things have a greater potential to destroy trust than conflict. Therefore organizations should prepare individuals to deal with conflict in ways that build rather than diminish trust.

When organizations take stock of themselves, most find that levels of trust are insufficient to bring about change. Trust has been allowed to deteriorate. A good way to restore trust is to combine quality conflict management with increased employee collaboration.

Trust in organizations must be both vertical and horizontal at every level. The following diagram illustrates this and shows the connection between trust and conflict. Research and experience indicate that levels of trust and quality of conflict management are directly proportional. High quality conflict resolutions yield high levels of trust.

DIMENSIONS OF TRUST

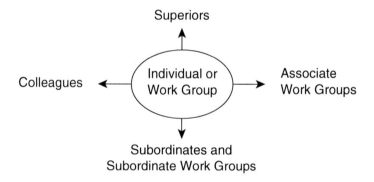

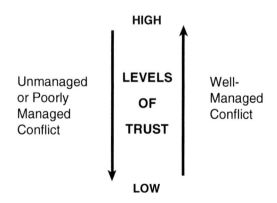

> Here is an interesting metaphor for trust. Think of trust as a house. It takes time to build a house. In most places about 120 days will do the job. Now you have a nice comfortable house that provides safety and shelter. It would take a skilled heavy-equipment operator only about 20 minutes to reduce this house to a pile of rubble. Now think about what a job it would be to restore this pile of rubble once again to that nice comfortable house and to do it so that no one would ever know that it had been destroyed.
>
> If you think about it, that's about what happens with trust when we're not careful with it.

Trust is a fragile asset. When we possess it either as individuals or organizations we are richer. Like any other asset, trust is a resource — an essential ingredient in quality relationships and organizations.

In their landmark book, *Leaders, Strategies for Taking Charge*, Warren Bennis and Burt Nanus say that "trust is the lubrication that makes it possible for organizations to work."

Considering its importance and value and its delicate nature, trust is not something to be trifled with, and yet, when individuals and organizations fail to adequately prepare themselves to effectively deal with conflict, that is precisely what they are doing.

Trust is the primary indicator by which we gauge the quality of any relationship. The degree to which we are willing to invest ourselves and our resources in a relationship is commensurate with the degree to which we feel trust.

TRY THIS!

Group Work (See Page 189)

Before discussing the role of trust in relationships, it is nice to have small groups work together to identify things they appreciate in some of their most important relationships. To facilitate this, use the topic, "The Attribute I Value Most in My Best Friend."

Here's an idea for elaborating —

Take a moment and think about one of your best friends. Try to fix in your mind some of the quality things that characterize this relationship. From these things select the attributes that come to mind and pick the one that you think is most valuable to you. Remember that an attribute is what a person is. What a person does (behavior) is an outgrowth of his or her attributes. Our topic is, "The Attribute I Value Most in My Best Friend."

Give everyone time to share and then facilitate a discussion with the following questions:

— *Of what importance are these traits in establishing relationships?*

— *How do we select people with whom to establish relationships?*

Since interpersonal conflict is a natural consequence of any relationship, and since trust determines the strength of any relationship and conflict more than anything else influences trust, then being able to manage relational conflict well is essential to maintaining and nurturing relationships.

TRY THIS!

Group Work (See Page 189)

You can further amplify the value of trust by considering what happens to relationships, both personal and professional, when trust is violated. To promote this understanding, you may wish to use the powerful topic, "A Time Someone Betrayed My Trust."

Here's an idea for elaborating —

Sometimes in life we must deal with the disappointment of having someone we trust or have confidence in let us down. This can be someone we know well or even intimately, or it can be a public figure, role model, colleague, or someone we otherwise admire. Think of a time when you were let down, lost confidence, or felt that your trust had been betrayed. You don't need to tell us who this person is or even what they do, but if you'd like, explain the situation and how you felt. The topic is, "A Time Someone Betrayed My Trust. "

When everyone has shared who would like to, facilitate a discussion with the following questions:

— *How are our relationships affected in these situations?*

— *When things like this happen, how long do the effects last?*

In an organizational context, relationships are often cast in terms of work groups or teams. For a team to fulfill the measure of its creation, it must possess high levels of trust. In fact, trust is a hallmark of any successful team. It is not only important, it is essential. What incentive does a person have to put 100 percent into a team effort when he or she doesn't trust that others on the team will do the same? The absence of trust in a group breeds suspicion and cynicism that, at best, causes us to withhold commitment and, at worst, promotes sabotage.

> Trust is a hallmark of any successful team. It is a team's greatest source of creative energy. It is not only important, it is essential!

Over the years, I have promoted the idea that conflict is also a necessary ingredient in the culture of successful teams. If, as has been suggested, conflict is the seed of creativity, then teams need conflict to produce creative results.

Why else do we have teams if not to combine diverse points of view to produce optimal results? The only way to avoid conflict on a team is to have no diversity, which is impossible. If it were possible, it would be counterproductive.

Being able to manage conflict is at once the mortar that holds teams together and the gateway to the creative energy that allows them to be productive.

> Being able to manage conflict is at once the mortar that holds teams together and the gateway to the creative energy that allows them to be productive.

Here is a scenario we often find in organizations today: By design or necessity, an organization starts to "flatten" (dismantle its outmoded hierarchical structure in favor of a broader, more flexible sharing of authority and responsibility.) This metamorphosis calls for the formation of work and decision-making teams at all levels in the organization. Often by mandate, these teams are expected to represent the entire corporate culture. They bring together middle managers, professional/technical staff, support personnel, and others.

Organizations all over the country have moved in this direction. In virtually no case, however, has adequate attention been given to readying people to work together in these collaborative settings.

TRY THIS!

To help people get a grasp of the challenges of moving to highly collaborative models, conduct a brainstorming session asking the participants: "What issues arise when we put together project teams or other groups with broad organizational representation?"

As people share, make a list on the board or chart paper. When no more ideas are offered, facilitate a discussion with the following questions:

— *What outcomes might develop if we fail to effectively manage these issues? (answers should include distrust, ineffectiveness, etc.)*

— *What will likely accrue if we succeed in managing existing issues and the conflicts that arise along the way?*

In most transformational efforts, the various players have already developed varying levels of mutual distrust. Many hourly workers, for example, are intimidated by both their immediate supervisors and department managers. Similarly, line supervisors may feel threatened by a handful of experienced workers and may distrust certain managers. Finally, managers are often called on to share power with those they have avoided empowering in the past. A long history of adversarial relations between labor and management and initiatives promoted by special interest and vocal minority groups can, and very often do, combine to create such high levels of suspicion and low levels of trust that the effort is doomed from the beginning.

Virtually every effort at transforming an organization is plagued by a degree of distrust. Distrust is an enormous impediment to success. Given this fact, why do so few such initiatives call for preparing people to handle change effectively?

Will we ever learn that conflict is inevitable and that the vast majority of people are not equipped to deal with it as effectively as they might, and that poorly managed conflict consumes our resources, produces distrust, destroys our best laid plans, and is TOTALLY within our ability to manage?

This question may be our greatest organizational paradox.

Advocacy — Factions versus Coalitions

One way to determine where an organization is with respect to its ability to effectively manage conflict is to examine the extent to which it is characterized by either coalitions or factions. Both accurately reflect the organization's culture.

Coalitions suggest a culture of collaboration and trust. Factions indicate distrust and discord.

Factions are groups of individuals who have joined together, most often informally, within the larger organization in support of particular ideas or beliefs. They are usually contentious and often disruptive in support of these ideas or beliefs and very often engage in political maneuvering or even sabotage to further their position. All this works to pull an organization apart.

Though factions exist within the organization, in a real sense they operate outside the organization, at odds with its purposes, policies, and procedures. When a group does not contribute to the well-being of the organization, it is taking away from it.

To the extent that factions are present in an organization, we see varying degrees of conflict and, in turn, an organizational culture characterized by high levels of political intrigue and distrust. We see conflict managing the organization.

Coalitions develop when organizations are successful in bringing together factions and other groups within the larger organization and redirecting their energy toward productive outcomes.

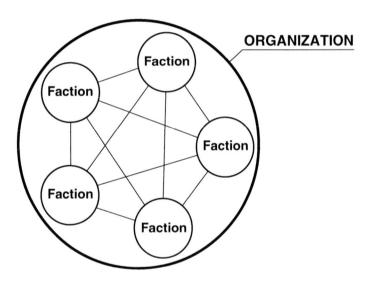

The truth is that organizations will always have factions. They come and go as change occurs and interest in ideas and attendant beliefs ebbs and flows. The problem for an organization develops when factions are not supplanted by coalitions. By themselves, factions operate to the detriment of the organization. When brought into coalitions, they can be transformed into contributing and productive elements of the organization.

It is important to remember that all organizations are characterized by both formal and informal structures. The former are reflected in the organizational chart and delineate authority and responsibility. The latter are structures that evolve as we put people into positions created within the formal organization. Sometimes informal structures form as ways of productively expediting the performance of tasks and responsibilities. This is good and is often followed by organizational redesign to formalize these structures.

Often, however, informal structures develop that are counter to productivity and the general well-being of the organization. These are factions, and are always part of the informal organization.

Good managers and leaders are able to perceive the development of factions and redirect their energies into productive channels. They do this by developing coalitions. But how is this done?

In two ways. The first involves the group leader or manager who has developed the skills of conflict management and coupled these with an understanding and mastery of the skills of advocacy or what we'll refer to in section six as advocacy by initiative.

Since conflict is inherent in the formation of a faction, the leader/manager must first be able to stabilize this conflict long enough to redirect its energy in appropriate ways. This requires both time and skill. It requires that the leader/manager first identify the faction; second, establish a trust-building dialogue with the faction; and finally, facilitate conflict resolution within the faction.

Next, the leader/manager must be able to create a means by which the faction can productively realign itself with the purposes of the organization and at the same time get an acceptable level of what it wants. This is accomplished as the leader/manager successfully advocates for the faction with other factions and groups within the organization and subsequently builds coalitions. Again this takes both significant time and skill.

Two questions must now be asked. First, do leaders and managers possess the skills required to facilitate in this manner? And, second, do they have the time to build coalitions and still fulfill their primary responsibilities?

The second approach to coalition-building involves the leader/manager who, understanding that factions will form and that coalition-building is essential, prepares his or her people to deal effectively in both conflict and advocacy, and in so doing allows them to better manage and advocate for themselves in these situations.

The leader/ manager will still need to invest time and skill in facilitating these outcomes, but to a much lesser extent. In addition, the factions themselves, because they now have an awareness and skill base, will consume less time and energy in the shift from faction to coalition. These savings begin almost immediately and over the long term can be substantial.

Since the first option requires the leader/manager to essentially start over again with each new faction, the time and energy consumed compounds with each new situation. The second option should be the clear choice. Both the leader/manager and his or her people experience growth and are better prepared to handle not just those issues that develop factions, but all the things that generate conflict. Moreover, the time and energy conserved represent significant resource savings.

Resource consumption

Leader/manager intervenes as need becomes apparent and facilitates conflict management and advocates for faction.

Resource Savings (Conservation)

Leader/manager assists people in developing the skills of conflict management and advocacy beforehand and facilitates as required.

Disadvantage —

Process must be repeated for each situation resulting in dependence on leader/manager's intervention and enormous resource consumption.

Benefit —

Each facilitation experience reinforces skills and builds competencies for both the leader/ manager and his or her people.

When we consider resources, anything we can do to conserve them operates to our advantage both as individuals and organizations.

Anything we can do to conserve resources operates to our advantage both as individuals and organizations. Furthermore, as we are better able to take charge of conflict within the organization, trust, innovation and creativity —the generative aspects of conflict — become irrepressible secondary outcomes.

THE EVOLUTION OF CONFLICT

In any setting, the sources of conflict are the same and ultimately involve issues related to comfort zones. Regardless of what comfort-zone issue sets the wheels of conflict in motion, once in gear conflict has the capacity to move into a dominant position quickly.

When the process of conflict begins, it moves inexorably toward resolution. The quality of the resolution depends almost entirely on the skills brought to bear during the management of the conflict.

The Stages of Conflict

> When the process of conflict begins, it moves inexorably toward resolution. The quality of this resolution depends almost entirely on the skills brought to bear in its management.

Conflicts come in all sizes. One way of characterizing a conflict is to measure its emotional intensity. The way we interpret what we perceive determines our emotions. If we perceive a threat to any of those areas we identified earlier as sources of conflict, then to some extent emotions are triggered. The greater the threat the greater the emotional intensity attached to the conflict.

We deal with conflict continuously, but for the most part everyday conflicts are small and have little emotional consequence. However, as conflict escalates, concern for self increases, and with it mechanisms of self-protection.

Sometimes conflicts become more serious — they distract us and generate fear, anger, or disappointment. These feelings are the conscious awareness we get when a conflict has higher emotional intensity. As self-interest increases, so does the desire to "win" and to save face.

Less often, we experience conflicts that produce intense feelings that reflect equally intense emotional content. As the emotional intensity of conflict increases, it becomes increasingly difficult to keep the conflict under control. In fact, conflicts can intensify to the point of being uncontrollable.

In this book, the little upsetting things that happen to us daily are labeled Stage One Conflicts. Conflicts that produce stronger feelings of discomfort that tend to distract us from what it is we would normally be doing are referred to as Stage Two Conflicts.

Finally, those conflicts that cause us to lose control are called Stage Three Conflicts. This escalation of feelings is directly related to the behaviors we exhibit at each stage. Though the feelings may be similar for all of us, the ways we manifest those feelings (our behaviors) vary widely.

Conflicts, when poorly managed, tend to escalate easily and sometimes quickly through these stages.

Conflicts can also skip stages. A person can move from level-headed to near berserk without stopping in between. A person given to violent outbursts is sending a danger signal that he or she lacks self-discipline and self-control. No organization should fail to take notice.

TRY THIS!

As a way of helping others more clearly understand the stages of conflict, refer to the activity beginning on Page 41. Here, you created a list of distractions people were experiencing that were getting in the way of their performance. Using this list, ask the individuals who volunteered their distractions to judge whether their distraction(s) was a Stage One or Stage Two Conflict. As the determinations are made, indicate by placing a "1" or "2" next to the distraction in the space you left blank along the right margin.

Ask other participants to reflect on their distractions and make similar determinations for themselves.

Facilitate a discussion by asking this question:

– *What does it take to have one of these distractions escalate into a Stage Two or Stage Three Conflict?*

Predicaments and Unresolvables

When a conflict reaches Stage Three, the situation is not only critical, but it can be characterized as a *predicament*. A predicament is a situation that is out of control (not beyond control) and in which control must be reestablished before management can begin or resume.

Unmanaged or poorly managed conflicts tend to escalate.

Contrasting a predicament with a problem is simple. We can solve problems, we can only control predicaments; however, when we gain control of a predicament it begins to transform itself into a problem and in so doing lends itself to management and resolution.

Though all Stage Three Conflicts are predicaments, not all predicaments are Stage Three Conflicts. Sometimes Stage Two and even Stage One Conflicts can be predicaments. These predicaments are called unresolvables — seeming to defy resolution. They are situations in which individuals and groups are simply unable to move from the position that puts them in conflict to one where resolution is possible. Often these situations offer us few choices, since actions are dictated by rule or regulation.

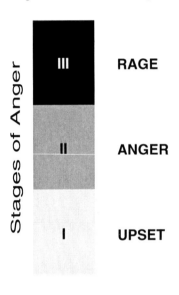

Stages of Anger

III   **RAGE**

II   **ANGER**

I   **UPSET**

In organizations, resolution of these kinds of conflicts is often accomplished with the simple expedient of changing things — reorganizing a department, effecting a transfer, adopting new policies, changing job assignments or responsibilities, etc. Virtually all organizational change flows from conflict. But anybody that has dealt with change will also tell you that all change produces conflict. So when organizations use change to deal with predicaments, they are simply replacing one conflict with another. Many times the new conflicts are resolvable and this gives the impression that change is a useful way of dealing

The extent to which organizational resources are wasted because of ill-concieved change is incalculable.

with conflict. But at what cost? Sometimes these emerging conflicts are worse, like jumping from the frying pan into the fire. The extent to which organizational resources are wasted because of ill-conceived change is incalculable, yet this is the strategy of choice for many organizations.

THE IMPACT OF CRISIS

A crisis is what develops when we move from a Stage Two to a Stage Three Conflict. By definition, a crisis is a turning point; however, in conflict the connotation is usually negative. The implication is that once a situation reaches the crisis point it is at the brink of turning ugly.

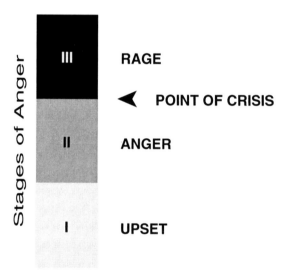

Obviously, the best way of dealing with crisis is to avoid it in the first place. Up to this point, we've talked about the nature and dynamics of conflict with just this idea in mind. Unfortunately, the potential for crisis always exists regardless of the work done to prevent it and, however well prepared we may be, we will be involved in crises from time to time.

Understanding this, it's up to us to decide how we want to approach a crisis. If a crisis is indeed a turning point, it can have a positive as well as negative outcome. The determining factor is the aplomb with which we deal with the crisis. Like any other conflict situation, good management is more likely to produce a desirable outcome than poor management or no management at all.

TRY THIS!

Group Work (See Page 189)

So that people can connect with the intensity and gravity of the crisis situation, have them explore one from their own frame of reference using the topic, "A Time I Observed or Was Involved in a Crisis Level Conflict."

Here's an idea for elaborating —

Directly or indirectly, almost everyone has experienced crisis. Take a moment and think of a crisis you've either been involved with or observed. It may have been one you experienced on the job, in a public place, or even at home. Remember, a crisis doesn't necessarily involve anger. It can involve illness, accident, economic concerns, fear, and many other emotions. Take some time to think carefully about your experience and then, if you like, share with the group a little about the incident, some of what went on for you in terms of feelings and behavior, and what outcome was generated. Our topic is, "A Time I Observed or Was Involved in a Crisis Level Conflict."

When everyone who wants to has shared, ask the following questions:

— *What kinds of feelings do we experience during crisis? . . . What behaviors can we expect on the part of people directly or indirectly involved in the situation?*

— If crises were dealt with more effectively, in what ways could the outcomes be improved?

If you are working with more than one small group, after the groups have finished, generate a large group discussion about the consequences of crisis when it is allowed to slip into Stage Three Conflict, and the possibilities when it is moved back to Stage Two.

Surprisingly, the first step in dealing with crisis is simply to recognize it for what it is. Too often we are blind-sided by situations that catch us so off guard that it is almost impossible to recover. When this happens, results are almost always negative. Since lack of recognition is the most common failing in crisis prevention, and since results are almost always negative, it's easy to see why crises receive such bad press. Hardly anybody says, "Wow, a crisis, what a great opportunity!"

Taken to the extreme, the failure to recognize a potential crisis can be deadly. According to national statistics, fifteen people die every week from violence in the workplace that is considered preventable. Nice people become harmful to others as conflict escalates; we don't see the danger coming because we're not familiar with their behaviors under the intense stress of stage three conflict.

Offices and other work settings (and not just in the inner-city) are increasingly settings for these kinds of incidences. The purpose of this book, however, is not to address just this extreme, but to focus on the fact that crises can have disastrous consequences that go far beyond the human resource implications, and that for the most part they can be dealt with far better than they currently are.

If recognition is the first step, how do we achieve it?

It's not easy to climb inside the psyche of an individual or the collective psyche of a group, either of which can be a player in crisis. Most of us don't know how we'll respond in an emotionally charged situation. To know what triggers another person's behaviors is almost impossible.

Given this problem, how are we to identify a potential crisis?

> **Every conflict situation contains the seeds of crisis, the key is to examine the conflict and not the participants.**

Since every conflict situation contains the seeds of crisis, the key is to examine the conflict and not the participants. Most of the time we evaluate a conflict based on the behaviors we see. If the behavior is aggressive, we tend to think the conflict is more serious than if the behavior is passive. The level of aggression is not a reliable indicator of the seriousness of the situation. A person who exhibits passive behaviors may be storing emotional energy, like a time bomb waiting to explode.

At either extreme, passive or aggressive, the behavior is less important as an indicator than is the situation.

The degree to which a conflict is a threat to the safety, security, self-esteem, control, or even love that an individual experiences tells us more than does the individual's behavior. Remember that we have all developed certain styles for responding to conflict. We've shaped these automatic responses over the years as ways of protecting ourselves from perceived threat. They are not always accurate indicators of what we are likely to do next. On the other hand, the psychology of the situation is almost universal in its implications. Going back to the need hierarchy of Abraham Maslow, we can see that all of us are influenced in predictable ways by the extent to which we perceive that certain needs are threatened or unmet. The situations that produce these perceptions vary widely, as do our responses.

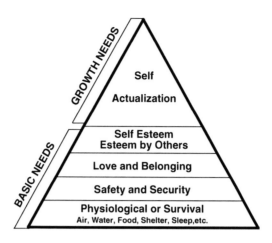

As we examine the hierarchy, we see that all the sources of conflict we discussed earlier can be found among Maslow's Basic Needs. In the context of crisis, looking at the situation and the extent to which it threatens the individual is of greatest value in controlling a crisis. The behaviors need only be dealt with if they represent a threat to the individual or those around him or her.

It's important to note that the lower the hierarchical level, the greater the perceived threat. The message here is, don't spend too much time trying to figure out what people are likely to do, rather spend more time in understanding the situation and how it's affecting them.

> Don't spend too much time trying to figure out what people are likely to do, rather spend more time in understanding the situation and how it's affecting them.

Remember, too, that what's been said here holds true for groups as well. In crisis prevention, we teach people to understand situations and the range of possible responses first, and then move to develop strategies for dealing with crisis should it result. This means presuming that some kinds of conflict have a greater chance of developing into crises and then adequately preparing for these possibilities.

A workplace example of crisis can be found in the employee who, for whatever reason, feels that he or she is being dealt with unfairly, and perceives this as a significant personal threat or affront, which turns the situation into a highly-charged emotional event. Whatever else may be the case, this individual is cast in a Stage Two Conflict. Depending on the person's conflict management style, he or she will deal with this situation in ways that are no longer safe to predict. The news is full of workplace tragedies where this kind of scenario played itself out in violence. But keep in mind that cases like these are the extreme.

Ninety-nine-point-nine percent of the time or more, the outcome does not involve violence. Because of this, most organizations seem to think that the risk is acceptable. Statistics don't support this thinking. But even if they did, the less visible and nonviolent results of crisis can be disastrous.

Whenever a crisis is allowed to develop in an organization, the disruption it creates absorbs incredible resources. Every act of sabotage, every slow down in production, every withholding of information or creative thinking is a symptom of a crisis. The truth is, most organizations are full of latent crises that leaders and managers are taking great pains to suppress in the belief that if they can just keep the lid on it, in time it will go away. In most cases they are right. However, in the time it takes for a crisis to go away, irreparable damage is often done and irreplaceable resources are consumed for nothing. Time heals all wounds — but at what cost?

> It is far more important and productive to develop in leader/managers the ability to recognize the potential for crisis and how to head it off than it ever will be to only train them in how to deal with a crisis once it manifests itself.

Developing in leaders/managers the ability to recognize the potential for crisis and head it off is far more important than merely training them in how to deal with a crisis once it exists. Here again, an ounce of prevention prevails.

SUMMARY

Only after we look at the consequences or effects of conflict are we really able to determine the value of preparing individuals to be effective in dealing with it. Understanding that unmanaged or poorly managed conflicts always produce negative results is the first step. Being aware that conflicts exist on a continuum that ranges from minor disagreements to major confrontations and even violence is important to the recognition that optimum conflict management results in win-win resolutions and that anything less involves applying conflict management to the minimization of losses. Well managed conflicts produce positive change and personal growth that can ultimately reshape the culture of an organization.

Conflict is directly connected to individual, group and organizational productivity as it impacts self-esteem, quality and, most importantly, resources. It influences the culture of the organization in another critical way. It bears directly on levels of trust among individuals, groups, and throughout the entire organization.

Organizations spawn factions that tend to favor self-interest over organizational interest. Advocacy becomes the strategy of choice as managers successfully redirect the energy drawn from the organization by factions into the formation of coalitions and larger collaborative groups.

To complete the examination of the dynamics of conflict, it is vital to understand how conflict evolves. This understanding begins with an examination of the three stages of conflict and ways in which people tend to behave at each stage. As conflicts escalate, which they tend to do when left unmanaged, they can turn into predicaments that defy resolution. Although predicaments can and must be controlled, they possess only the potential for resolution. Predicaments occur in Stage Three Conflicts. Only by taking control of Stage Three Conflicts can we are transform predicaments into problems that lend themselves to resolution.

Unless controlled, predicaments remain unresolvable, however not all unresolvables are predicaments. We find unresolvables in both Stage One and Two Conflicts as well. Unresolvables are conflict situations in which individuals and/ or groups are unwilling or unable to move to positions that allow room for resolution. Having the ability to recognize unresolvables helps individuals and groups move beyond them. Unresolvables can be veritable "black holes," continuously absorbing valuable resources.

When a conflict moves from Stage Two to Stage Three, it becomes a crisis. Understanding the nature of crisis and how to approach it is critical to the management of those conflicts which have the potential of producing the most devastating results.

Conflict has as much potential for producing positive results as it does for generating negative results. The difference is what we bring to each conflict situation.

TAKING CHARGE OF
ORGANIZATIONAL CONFLICT

4. THE NATURE OF CONFLICT

Having an awareness of the physiology and psychology of conflict is a critical first step toward becoming an effective conflict manager. Understanding what's happening to us when we are in conflict is the key to maintaining conscious control of ourselves as we confront conflict situations. Too often, we treat this step as though it were superfluous, moving immediately into processes. This is a huge mistake, because it assumes that people are ready to engage in successful conflict management. Nothing is farther from the truth. The minute people start to understand what's happening to them, they are better able to do something about it. Understanding the nature of conflict — how it affects us as individuals — is a vital prerequisite to conflict management.

> **Think about this . . .**
>
> Some of the people in our lives we choose to be there and they are the objects of our affection like close friends and spouses. With some we even have a hand in their creation like our children. Even with all this, we still have conflicts. How can we expect to have no conflicts with the people with whom we work when we can't always get along with those we choose, love, and create?

There are few things that we can say for sure, but one of them is that all of us will experience conflict in our lives from time to time. It's part of living in a world with other people. In fact, we would encounter conflict even if we were the only person alive on the planet, because we not only have conflict with others, we have conflict with ourselves. Think of a time when you had to make a tough decision. Part of you said, "yes" and another part said, "no." You were in conflict. In fact, it could be argued that conflict begins even before we are born (does the unborn really want to leave the womb?) and continues until we take our last breath, reluctantly yet resignedly letting go of life.

When we hear the word conflict, most of us respond by thinking of something negative. The words the dictionary chooses to define conflict tend to support this inclination; words like carnage, destruction, battle, warfare, fight, and so on. Why is it that we rarely associate conflict with positive words and images? For example, when we achieve a resolution between two conflicting ideas we call that an agreement. Maybe conflict can be seen as an opportunity for agreement. Now that's something positive!

TRY THIS!

With a group of any size conduct a word association activity.

Ask group participants to volunteer as many words as they can think of that are synonyms for the word *conflict.*

Make a list and you will see the negative connotation conflict has developed.

You can use this list to start a discussion of the differences between the process of conflict and its consequences (outcomes).

When we start thinking about conflict as opportunity, we soon see that all the negative connotations we've associated with conflict in the past really only describe the outcomes of poorly resolved or unresolved conflict. Conflict by itself is neither good nor bad, it just is. However, when conflict goes unmanaged and unresolved, it can turn into some pretty ugly things, as the dictionary attests.

> Conflict by itself is neither good nor bad, it just is.

You've heard the adage, "Opportunity seldom knocks twice." Well, the fact is, opportunity rarely knocks at all, and it certainly doesn't arrive heralded by banners and drum rolls. True, there's a world of opportunity out there, but we have to *find* it, and many times it's disguised as conflict. In fact, in Mandarin Chinese, the word *conflict* means "opportunity riding on a dangerous wind."

Thinking about conflict as opportunity, and understanding that poorly resolved or unresolved conflict can lead to negative and destructive outcomes, opens the doors to a whole new way of looking at and learning from conflict.

Most people think of conflict as an event or condition involving more than one person or group. But whether conflict involves other people or is an inner struggle to reach a decision or resolve an issue, conflict begins in the mind. In the past few years, we've learned much about the way the mind functions. From the cognitive neurosciences, we have begun to see the connections between our perceptions and responses to what goes on around us.

Every human being exists in an environment. We are surrounded by that environment our entire lives, and we are also part of it. That is, the environment is both outside of us and inside of us. Let's examine this relationship more closely using the following model:

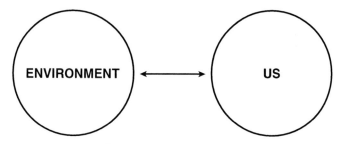

The arrow between the two circles represents the relationship we have with our various environments. The relationship is two way. We affect the environment and the environment affects us. We actually have three primary environments. The first and most familiar to us is our external environment. We connect with this environment through our senses (*i.e.*, taste, touch, smell, hearing and sight). The totality of nature, the physical environment in which we work and live, and all other people and objects with which we interact are part of this environment.

Next, is our body environment. We connect to our body through our nervous system, which gives us all kinds of feedback. We know when we're ill or have been injured, when we need more rest or get too much, when we've eaten too much or too little, etc.

> We live in three environments simultaneously. All profoundly affect us.

Finally, we have our own thoughts. Our thinking is capable of producing its own environment. Have you ever been so engrossed in thought that you lost touch with what was going on around you? Things were happening, but you didn't notice because you were absorbed with your own thinking.

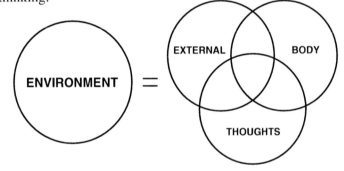

These three environments all combine and interact to shape our world.

> While we may all share similar environments, no two of us is alike. We all have beliefs, traits, and ways of doing things that make us forever unique.

The other half of the relationship is ourselves, and while we may all share similar environments, no two of us are alike. Over time, we all have accumulated information and with it have formed the basis for what we believe and value. These beliefs and values help shape our perceptions, determine our judgements, and govern our behavior. Collectively they are called our belief systems.

Along with our belief systems we also have human traits. These are things like temperament, personality, learning style and even the nature of our intelligence, to name a few. In addition, we also have certain conditioned responses that have been developed over time. We often refer to these as habits of behavior. They're the things we do without thinking — the ways we naturally go about leading our lives. Taken together, our beliefs, traits, and habits define us as unique individuals. They define who we are.

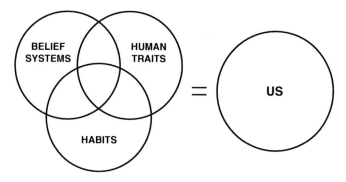

Because we believe differently, have different human traits, and have our own ways of doing things (habits), we are truly unique. As such, we perceive our environment uniquely. As much as seventy percent of all that we perceive, we see differently than others because our perceptions are uniquely shaped by who we are — our habits, beliefs, and traits. The following activity demonstrates this.

TRY THIS!

Write the following statement in all capital letters on a chalk board or chart pad, or create an overhead transparency:

FINISHED FILES ARE THE
RESULT OF YEARS OF SCIENTIFIC
STUDY COMBINED WITH THE
EXPERIENCE OF MANY YEARS

Read the statement to the group. Have participants, without talking to one another or speaking out, simply count the number of "F"s that appear in the statement. While they are counting read the statement to them one more time.

Allow a reasonable amount of time (not more than 30 seconds); then remove the statement so that it is no longer visible to the group. Ask participants to indicate by a show of hands if they saw only three "F"s in the statement. Count the raised hands, and record this number so that everyone can see it. Now ask those who saw only four "F"s to raise their hands. Again, count and record. Ask those who saw only five "F"s in the statement to raise their hands. Record this number. Finally, ask for a show of hands from those who saw only six "F"s in the statement. Record this number.

Mention that there certainly seems to be some disagreement.

Repeat the entire process, but only allow 15 seconds for participants to recount the "F"s, and again remove the statement from view. Record the new responses next to the original numbers and note the changes. After completing the second group poll, point out that there is still disagreement. Now return the statement so that it can be seen by everyone and lead a group count of the six "F"s that appear in the statement.

Facilitate a discussion by asking the following questions:

— *Why was it that even after counting the "F"s twice and suspecting that all was not as it appeared to be, we still had so much disagreement?*

We can already see how, just by being unique and perceiving things differently, we have the makings of conflict.

DIVERSITY AND CONFLICT

According to the dictionary, something that is *diverse* is "made up of distinct characteristics or qualities." Using that definition as a measure, scarcely an organization in existence fails to qualify as diverse. Put two or more people together and you have diversity. It goes with the organizational territory. Everyone walks to different drumbeat, hears through a different filter, and sees through a different lens.

BLOCKERS VS. ENHANCERS

Unfortunately, the notion of diversity within organizations isn't often linked to "distinct qualities and characteristics," which in and of itself is politically neutral, but instead to the avoidance of politically incorrect biases having to do with age, gender, race, ethnicity, and culture. Legalized "quota systems" mandate particular forms of diversity — often superficial — thereby giving the concept of diversity its largely negative connotation.

> Diversity should always be thought of as an asset and never as an issue. When diversity is an issue, all the magic goes out of it and only ugliness is left.

Ask around. Diversity is rarely viewed as an asset. Executives and middle managers see it as essential to obtaining grants and funding, placating segments of the community, maintaining good public relations, and avoiding lawsuits. Many workers see it as a threat to their job security.

Achieving racial, ethnic, and gender balance through real or perceived quota systems; implementing policies that "protect" employees from sexual harassment while bringing about the extinction of cross-gender compliments; retaining an inept employee to avoid a potential lawsuit — all of these practices act as *blockers*. They prevent managers and employees from recognizing the true benefits of diversity. At worst they create animosity and resentment; at best they fool bureaucrats into believing that something meaningful has occurred.

Blockers can totally obscure the real benefits of diversity. Racial, ethnic, gender, and age differences are often viewed as issues within an organization — seeds of conflict — rather than as assets. Organizational leaders need to help people look beyond these blocking issues to see the *enhancers* inherent in diversity.

WHAT ARE ENHANCERS?

Enhancers are such things as ideas, beliefs, knowledge, experience and intellect. In order to appreciate these *defining* products of diversity, people have to do something that isn't required in the vast majority of organizations, and in some is subtly discouraged. They have to get to know each other. Knowledge and appreciation of enhancers is an outgrowth of the rapport developed between people. It's the fruit of relationships.

Beliefs. A belief is a learned conviction about the truth, actuality, or validity of something. Everyone possesses a collection of beliefs, and each person's collection is unique and changing.

Beliefs range from simple to complex. Simple beliefs require modest intellectual understanding. (The sun comes up in the morning. Vegetables are good for you.) Complex beliefs tend to be made up of combinations of simple beliefs. No wonder people have trouble explaining what they believe. *They just believe it.*

Some beliefs are reasonable, others unreasonable. For example, the greatest fear reported by a majority of Americans is fear of public speaking. People with this fear *believe* that something terrible will happen to them if they stand up before an audience and attempt to express themselves. While this may not be an unreasonable belief for some, the fact that it's number one *is* unreasonable. That it inspires greater trepidation than such things as job loss, mugging, cancer, or traffic accidents is absurd!

Our beliefs can put us in conflict when we try to impose them on others. Because we take our beliefs very personally and cling to them tightly, a lively discussion can spiral into intense debate and then into conflict simply because one person's "right" belief makes the other person "wrong." If we'd stop to think how rigorously we protect and defend our own beliefs, we'd recognize the unfairness and futility of expecting others to roll over while we stomp all over theirs. They won't. Unless we're dealing with a person who is skilled enough to remain emotionally detached, conflict *will* ensue.

A belief doesn't change just because someone tells us — or even "proves" to us — that we are wrong. It changes when the emotional experience on which it is based is replaced by a more powerful emotional experience producing a new belief. For example, if the fear of public speaking is based on real experiences involving embarrassment, humiliation or loss of self-esteem, logic and reasoning will not make that fear go away. However, by planning, carefully, preparing and repeatedly rehearsing our next speech, we may be able to create an experience that generates pride, satisfaction, and heightened self-esteem. And if we repeat and thereby reinforce this new experience several times over a period of weeks or months, our belief about public speaking is likely to be transformed.

The varying beliefs of individuals within an organization are like a field of diamonds waiting to be discovered. Until we recognize and understand the wealth inherent in that field, we're not likely to examine a single rock. We'll just keep throwing them at each other.

Habits. Habits — both positive and negative — are learned through conditioning. Driving an automobile, for example, involves a complex orchestration of learned behaviors that becomes habitual and unconscious with repeated practice.

Imagine what daily life would be like if we didn't form habits. We couldn't plan a meeting while jogging, think through a problem while folding laundry, or fantasize a perfect game of golf on the way to the course. By forming habits, we free up space for thinking. Having to think through every action would be highly inefficient.

Habits are a big source of conflict. A substantial number of people, it seems, have the habit of shaving time estimates to the barest minimum, thereby ensuring that they are frequently late for meetings and deadlines. The impact of chronic lateness sends out waves that can touch scores of people. Trivial behaviors like humming, popping gum, swearing, scratching, and sloppiness are initially matters of personal choice; however, as habits they exit the realm of conscious control and simultaneously shed their triviality. Other people react to such habits with everything from mild annoyance to extreme anger. But whether they simmer or seethe, they want us to stop *doing that!*

Yet as we all know, changing a habit is agonizingly difficult. Habitual behaviors are hard to stop because stopping them requires thinking about them, which is definitionally impossible. Habits exist parallel to but not within consciousness. Frequently, the best approach is to consciously learn new behaviors with the intent that they too become habitual and supplant the old behaviors. The process produces a one-step-forward, one-step-back dance with slow or no progress.

Traits. We are born with unique physical traits, and with a strong predisposition to certain behavioral and emotional traits as well. Eye and skin color, skeletal structure, the shape of the jaw or mouth are readily identifiable; emotional sensitivity, aggressiveness, athletic or artistic ability are revealed more slowly and recognized less often, but are distinguishable traits nonetheless. Each of us has a unique trait profile, with identical twins coming the closest to sharing traits.

Most traits, particularly physical ones, can't realistically be judged good or bad, and it's futile to try to mold others (children, spouse, friends, colleagues) into carbon copies of ourselves. Traits don't readily change; most are part of our genetic makeup. Furthermore, the desire for uniformity is folly. Sameness curtails creativity, retards productivity, and is simply dull.

Knowing how we resist the efforts of others to change us, we ought to realize that it is equally hard for us to change others. A few generations ago, left-handed children were commonly "trained" (intimidated, cajoled, punished) into becoming right-handed. Today, we still attempt to impose linguistic and logical/mathematical learning styles on individuals whose natural preference is to learn by some other method, such as hands-on experience. Force fits, if achieved at all, exact a high price.

Look again at the exercise on page 18. Typically, naming ways in which we are exactly alike produces a very short list, while specifying differences can cover pages. However, if we think in terms of the unifying aspects of our differences, we realize that they are linked by shared categories. One person may have smooth brown skin, another freckled pink skin, and another cool beige skin, but all have skin. One person sleeps on a bed, another on a futon, a third in a sleeping bag on the ground, but all sleep. Different cultures celebrate different holidays, but all celebrate. We don't have to look, think, or behave alike to be alike. Our humanness is a powerful unifying force.

The Flex Factor. Attempting change through directives is like trying to permanently reshape a rubber band by stretching it. Hold a rubber band in your right hand and stretch it out with your left. What happens when you let go with the left hand? The band snaps back. That's exactly what we do. We consciously stretch and begin to reshape ourselves, but when we let go, as we invariably do, we snap back to our old ways. What we want is a permanently stretched band, but how do we get it?

The Expansion Factor. Permanent expansion and change are achieved not through directives, but through learning. Learning allows us to value, recognize, and accommodate diversity.

Going back to our model, we can now see that our relationship with our environment is a dynamic one, and is unique to each individual. Since we are constantly interacting with our various environments, not only is the relationship dynamic, so is the quality of the relationship. And the quality produces feelings.

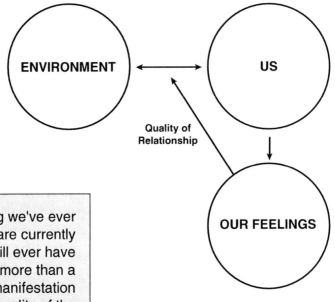

ENVIRONMENT ← → US

Quality of Relationship

OUR FEELINGS

> Every feeling we've ever had, are currently having, or will ever have is nothing more than a conscious manifestation of the quality of the relationship we're having with our environment.

Every feeling we ever have or will experience is nothing more than a conscious manifestation of the quality of the relationship we're having with our environment. It's not so much the environment as it is our perception of the environment that determines the quality. Our feelings are always accompanied by physical manifestations as well. Feelings and physical responses vary among individuals as much as individuals differ from each other.

COMFORT ZONES AND CONFLICT

As long as we see those elements that define us and our perceptions of the environment as being congruent, our world appears to be in harmony and we experience a sense of comfort. Whenever an incongruency appears in these relationships, we experience discomfort in the form of feelings and physical responses. A simple example has to do with driving speed. Each of us has a range of speed within which we are comfortable driving under specific conditions relative to traffic, visibility, weather, road conditions, etc. When we are forced to drive (or, as a passenger, ride) slower than the slowest speed in that range for more than a few minutes, we may feel impatient or agitated. At speeds higher than the highest speed in our comfort range, we may become tense, anxious, or fearful.

> Being out of our comfort zone arises from a disagreement between our beliefs and perceptions , and we have come to know this as conflict.

This relationship between defining factors and perceptions, and comfort and discomfort has given rise to the expression *comfort zone*. When things are in agreement with who we are, we say that we are in our comfort zone. When things don't agree, we experience discomfort and say that we are out of our comfort zone.

TRY THIS!

Group Work (See Page 189)

To help people make a personal connection between comfort zones and conflict use the topic, "A Conflict That I'm Currently Experiencing."

Here's an idea for elaborating —

Since conflict is an ongoing part of our lives, it should not be difficult to think of one with which you're currently dealing. It can be big or small, it can be personal or professional. Perhaps it involves others, or it might have to do with a difficult decision you must make. Select just one conflict and take a moment to reflect on how it is making you feel. If you'd like, share with the group a little about your conflict and your feelings. Again, the topic is, "A Conflict That I'm Currently Experiencing."

After everyone who would like to has had a chance to share, facilitate a discussion with the following question (record responses on a sheet of paper):

— *How do our conflicts make us feel?*

Now ask the group(s) to share some of the feelings they recorded. Create a list of these to refer to later in the activity on Page 85.

If being out of our comfort zone arises from a disagreement between the things that define us (beliefs, traits, habits)

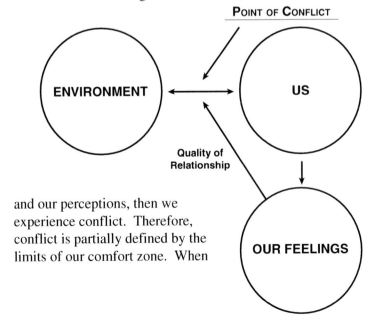

and our perceptions, then we experience conflict. Therefore, conflict is partially defined by the limits of our comfort zone. When we are in our comfort zone, we experience congruency, peace and harmony (an absence of conflict). When we approach the limits of our comfort zone, we begin to experience the feelings associated with conflict.

Since all feelings are generated as a result of the quality of our relationship with the environment, we can define this relationship as the point of conflict. All conflicts have to do with the quality of the relationship we're having with our environment.

CONFLICT AND STRESS

Another relationship we must be aware of is the one between conflict and stress.

TRY THIS!

Using this activity, create a degree of stress in participants as a way of helping them understand the relationship between conflict and stress.

Announce to the group that you're going to give them a short spelling test of only eight words, and that, as in other tests, you expect them to observe what would be considered good classroom behavior. Indicate that you will say each word once and then use it in a sentence. Also ask that the words be written in cursive.

As one final instruction, tell participants that you would like them to take the test using their non-dominant hand. That is, if they are right-handed, they are to use their left hand and so on. Note the responses of discomfort.

Begin the test using the following list of words:

Accommodate
Uncomfortable

Fortuitous
Inappropriate
Ambidexterity
Extraordinary
Ambiguity
Easy

Before inviting discussion, ask participants to help you make a list of the feelings they experienced either as you announced the test, instructed them to use their non-dominant hand, or administered the test.

After completing the list, circle the feelings that have a negative connotation. Now compare this list to the one you created when you completed the activity on Page 83, which involved a conflict participants were currently experiencing.

When we compare the feelings generated by a personal conflict with the ones generated by the spelling test, we see that they are essentially the same. The feelings of conflict are the same as the feelings of stress. Conflict and stress are synonymous. The feelings of stress are indicators that tell us we are in conflict.

Do adults experience stress? Absolutely. And like conflict, stress is a naturally occurring condition. This is important because the feelings we associate with stress alert us to the fact that something is happening in our environment that demands attention.

Additional facts about stress need to be considered. Like conflict, stress has been given a bad name these days, but that's because we have focused on only one kind of stress. There are actually three types of stress. The first is *eustress*, which is related to feelings of euphoria. We experience eustress when we have a peak experience — an experience accompanied by feelings of exhilaration, fulfillment and euphoria. In fact, the feelings of eustress actually define the peak experience. Eustress is good. It is therapeutic and healing.

The next type of stress is *hypostress*. This kind of stress is associated with high performance. When people say that they work better under stress, they are referring to hypostress. If you've ever been involved in a project or task and have lost track of time, not wanting to be disturbed, you've probably experienced hypostress. Hypostress is good. It produces positive energy and stimulates creativity.

It's the last type of stress that we make such a fuss over. *Distress.* In conflict, we experience feelings of distress. Whether the conflict has to do with our thoughts, a relationship with someone else, or a physical problem, the feelings are those of distress.

Stress is a label we put on various kinds of feelings. Some are good (those associated with eustress and hypostress) and some are bad (those associated with distress). The things in our environment that produce stress are called stressors. Those that produce distress are called distressors.

Now we can see that it's more correct to say that conflict and distress are synonymous. In fact, every conflict produces distress, and every cause of distress is a conflict. Whenever we perceive a situation to be at or beyond the limits of our comfort zone, we experience distress and are in conflict. You know you are reaching the limits of your comfort zone when you start having feelings of distress.

Looking again at our model on the next page, we can add that the point of conflict is also the point of stress:

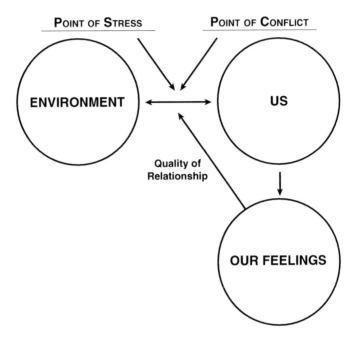

POINT OF STRESS   POINT OF CONFLICT

ENVIRONMENT   ←——→   US

Quality of
Relationship

OUR FEELINGS

MINDWORKS, STRESS, AND CONFLICT

Stress is a term we use to identify feelings. Distress is a category of negative feelings that we experience. Feelings are generated as each new perception of the environment is associated with previous information stored in our subconscious and is then evaluated based on its emotional significance and content. Here is another model that simplifies much of the new information flowing from the neurosciences that relates to the brain/mind complex and conflict. I call it Mindworks.

The brain and mind are separate. The brain is organic and the mind is systemic. Some researchers say that the mind is what the brain does. The Mindworks model is about what the mind does, not what it is.

Mindworks –

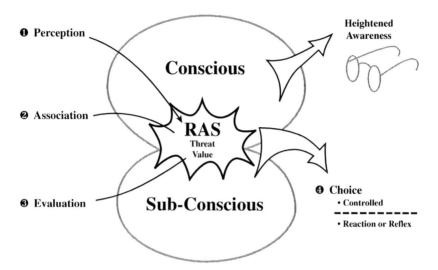

Our perceptions of the environment enter at the subconscious level. They provide encoded information to the Reticular Activating System or RAS (pronounced "rass"). By definition, reticular refers to a network and, in Mindworks, RAS networks with all the other operating systems of the mind.

As perceptions enter the reticular, RAS accesses memory information stored in the subconscious and the perceptions are then evaluated against all our prior learnings, experiences, beliefs, etc. Based on the collective emotional significance of this evaluation, RAS communicates with other operating systems at the subconscious level to generate physical responses and the feelings and thoughts we experience at the conscious level.

One of the important physical responses is a heightened awareness of the thing or things in the environment that stimulated the initial perception. This, in turn, produces additional perceptions that the reticular can use to better define the situation.

Some of our perceptions are associated with accumulated memories and prior experiences that suggest the existence of personal threat. When this happens we experience negative emotions like fear and jealousy. When a perception is evaluated as having negative emotional value, we experience negative feelings of distress.

As the emotional value of perceptions increases; that is, as we perceive greater threat, the intensity of our distress also increases.

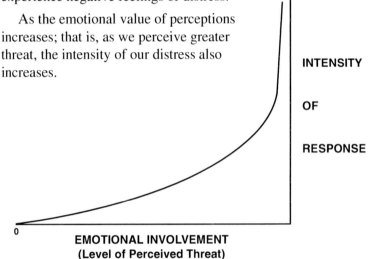

INTENSITY

OF

RESPONSE

0

EMOTIONAL INVOLVEMENT
(Level of Perceived Threat)

Not only do our feelings of distress intensify, but our physical responses also tend to become more intense. Going back to our earlier discussion of the stages of conflict, we can see that these stages are proportional to the level of emotional content.

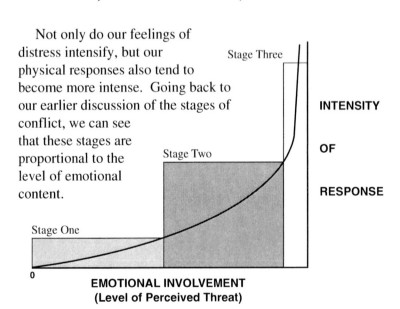

Stage Three

INTENSITY

Stage Two

OF

Stage One

RESPONSE

0

EMOTIONAL INVOLVEMENT
(Level of Perceived Threat)

Our responses become so intense in stage three that we lose control. This is the stage where individuals find themselves in predicaments requiring assistance as they try to restore control and regain the possibility of management.

Relating all of this to Maslow's Hierarchy of Needs, two things become apparent. First, all of the things in our environment that produce distress and therefore conflict fall into the general category of basic needs. Second, the farther down the hierarchy the distressor, the more significant the perceived threat, the greater the distress, and the more intense the response.

Pyramid labeled: GROWTH NEEDS / BASIC NEEDS. From top: Self Actualization; Self Esteem / Esteem by Others; Love and Belonging; Safety and Security; Physiological or Survival — Air, Water, Food, Shelter, Sleep, etc.

TRY THIS!

Group Work (See Page 189)

To illustrate the point that our distressors fall into the basic needs category, use the topic, "Something That Is Currently Causing Me Distress."

Here's an idea for elaborating —

Life presents us with many events that create feelings of stress. These are called stressors. Stressors can be people, events, situations, thoughts or even our wellness and health. Think of an example of something that is currently causing you to feel distress. If you choose, tell the rest of your circle group what it is that's causing you distress and what kinds of feelings you are experiencing. Select something to share and then take a few moments to reflect. The topic is, "Something That Is Currently Causing Me Distress."

After the sharing, facilitate small group discussions with the following question:

— *What kinds of feelings do we have when we are experiencing or thinking about one of our distressors?*

Post an illustration of Maslow's Hierarchy so that it can be seen by everyone. Now generate a large group discussion by asking a few individuals in the room to tell at what level on the Hierarchy of Needs they would place their distressor.

Anything we perceive as a threat to these basic needs not only produces distress, it puts us in conflict. Going back to the "us" in our original model, I want to reemphasize the role that our beliefs, human traits, and habits play in determining our perceptions.

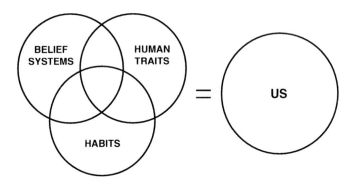

When RAS goes through its association and evaluation process in order to orchestrate our feelings and physical responses to an event, RAS accesses those things in the subconscious that make us unique. These are the things we've learned and come to believe; they're our conditioned responses, or habits; and finally, they are the traits that together distinguish us from every other human being. This explains why we perceive so many things differently than anyone else.

Whether small or large, conflicts occur when we perceive our environment being out of harmony with who we are. Through conflict, we attempt to restore that harmony. The habits we have formed and the skills we have acquired directly determine the results we produce any time we engage in conflict. Most of the time, these results are negative and that's why we have come to believe that conflict itself is negative. It is not. Conflict is a necessary part of living, and when engaged in with skill, almost always produces positive and satisfying results for everyone involved.

Even though we know better, most of us have, from time to time, found ourselves behaving poorly in conflict situations. Why is it that people do what they do when they know what they know? The answer is simple. Look again at the Mindworks model on Page 89. Focus on the conscious mind. This is a highly specialized system that really can do only one thing at a time. For example, it can't think and listen at the same time. So if you are distracted by your thoughts it is very difficult to listen with comprehension. An example of this we've all experienced is being introduced to someone for the first time and then realizing almost immediately that we can't remember the person's name. The primary functions of the conscious mind are cognitive and have to do with thinking and reasoning. Just as with RAS, the conscious mind perceives, associates, and evaluates, but its source of input is what flows to it from the subconscious.

Learning begins with the cognitive functions of the conscious mind. When real learning has been accomplished, the product of that learning takes residence in the unconscious mind. All beliefs and conditioned responses, all learnings, begin with conscious attention and then are turned over to the unconscious. All the things we do largely without thinking (i.e., walking and running, driving a car, hitting a ball, managing a conflict, etc.) were learned beginning with some conscious effort. The quality of that learning determines the quality or skill level of our behavior. Most people have not learned the best ways to deal with conflict and are left with habits that do not serve them well in conflict situations.

TRY THIS!

Group Work (See Page 189)

To allow people to explore their own conflict management habits use the topic, "How I React When I'm Angry."

Here's an idea for elaborating —

Everybody gets angry. When we get angry, we react in some way. Some of us shout, some of us stuff our anger deep inside us, some of us lash out at other people or things, and some of us throw and break things. How do you behave when you're angry? Maybe you dive into an activity of some kind and try to keep busy. Perhaps you're one of the many people who handle anger by withdrawing and becoming very silent. Or maybe you react verbally, saying things that you regret later. Think about this for a moment and, if you would like to share, the topic is, 'How I React When I'm Angry.'

After the sharing has concluded, start a discussion using the following questions:

— *How are Mindworks systems involved in the process of becoming angry?*

— *In what ways can we manage our conflicts better?*

Action versus Reaction.

Since the conscious mind is limited in the number of things it can do at once, the vast majority of our behavior is left to the unconscious to manage. Whatever the unconscious has learned to do it will do, unless overridden by deliberate conscious control. How many of us, for example, have driven somewhere and can't recall anything about the journey, or started out driving to one place and found ourselves going to another? We continue to do the things we have learned or been conditioned to do despite whatever we may know to the contrary unless we exercise conscious control. In this regard, knowledge is very different from learning. The automatic behavior generated by the unconscious (our habits) are reactions. To apply what we know to a situation requires conscious management or action.

This is the way we distinguish conflict management styles from conflict management strategies. Styles are our habitual ways of reacting, while strategies are our conscious and thoughtful ways of acting in a conflict situation. The vast majority of the time, we resort to our styles rather than strategies for two reasons. One, we are conditioned to react. Two, most of us have limited knowledge and skill when it comes to managing conflict. This is not to imply that our conflict styles are totally bad or inappropriate; however, most of us could do much, much better. Here are some common styles that people resort to in conflict:

Blaming others	-
Ignoring the situation	±
Resorting to secrecy	-
Threatening others	-
Fighting it out	-
Giving in	±
Repressing feelings	-
Trying to discover new possibilities	+

Getting angry	±
Complaining	-
Admitting differences	+
Admitting error, even when it is not believed	±
Changing the subject	±
Trying to understand other points of view	+

As you can see from the plus and minus signs on the right, some behaviors are almost always negative while others are always appropriate and positive. The remainder can be either positive or negative depending on the situation. By selecting those with plus signs we have the basis for starting to develop useful and constructive tools, approaches, and strategies that have great value when consciously and thoughtfully applied to resolving conflict.

THE GATEWAY SKILL

So... why do we do what we do when we know what we know? Because that which is *known* is competing against that which has been *learned*. Knowing something implies thought and cognition — a conscious process. A learning, as the term is used in psychology (particularly in behavior modification) is a habit or conditioned response. No thinking is required.

Knowing produces deliberate actions, which are sluggish compared to the swift conditioned responses that come from the unconscious. Triggered by our emotions, unconscious learned responses are lightning fast. By the time our conscious mind catches up, we're already in action — *behaving*, and sometimes badly. How many times have you had this experience: Your body is tense and flooded with feelings, your lips moving, words are coming out, and your conscious mind is watching, thinking, "There you go again," yet to stop the process feels like it will take superhuman effort. So you either observe, cognitively divorced from the process until it has run its course, or you allow yourself (your conscious, cognitive mind) to be drawn into the fray, as you begin to supply explanations and justification for your behavior.

These automatic responses to conflict are usually learned very early — as early as four years of age — and are emotionally driven. According to Daniel Goleman, author of the 1995 bestseller, *Emotional Intelligence*, all it takes is for some feature of a present conflict to resemble a conflict situation from the past. The instant that feature is recognized by the emotional mind, the feelings that went with the past event are triggered. The emotional mind reacts to the present *as if it were the past.* The reaction is fast and automatic, but not necessarily accurate or appropriate for the conflict at hand. Frequently we don't even realize what is happening.

What a breakthrough it would be if in that brief moment, that "gateway" before all hell breaks loose, we could seize control, stretch the moment, hold onto it, and override the feelings flowing from the unconscious long enough to *think* and to make reasoned choices. If we could say to ourselves, "No, I'm not going to be harnessed *once again* into this kind of response. I'm going to buy myself some time and think through a more appropriate response."

To accomplish this, we have to have a skill to use *in the gateway*. We might develop an arsenal of skills eventually, but we must have at least one, and it has to be a show-stopper. Ironically, once acquired, this gateway skill will eventually become a *new* habit, a *new* conditioned response, a *new* way to behave.

HOW TO RECOGNIZE THE GATEWAY MOMENT

Before we can use the gateway moment to gain conscious control in a conflict situation, we have to recognize that we have entered the gateway. If it were just a question of recognizing a conflict on the horizon, most of us would meet the challenge rather easily. The problem is, the lag time between recognition and cognitive response usually means that we're through the gateway and rushing headlong into our favorite rote emotional reaction before the gateway realization even registers.

It's like passing through a metal detector at the airport. Once you toss your carry-on items atop the conveyor belt it takes only seconds to step through the detector frame and continue on your way — unless the alarm goes off. What we need to do is rig an alarm to go off *every* time we step through the gateway that leads to conflict. We can do this if we configure our internal alarm mechanism to be highly sensitive to signs of *distress*. Distress signals the gateway moment.

TRY THIS!

To get in the habit of attending to the cognitive moment in conflict, keep a conflict journal for 30 days. Every time you become involved in any kind of a conflict, record the following information:

- Briefly describe the SITUATION.

- List as clearly and completely as possible, your FEELINGS.

- Describe what you said and did — your RESPONSE.

- Grade your response: - (negative)/ 0 (neutral) or/ + (positive).

CONFRONTATION

The point at which we begin the process of resolving a conflict is the point at which the conflict is confronted. This is a necessary first step in conflict management. Sometimes we initiate the confrontation, other times the situation brings on the confrontation, and still other times someone else initiates the confrontation.

The best situation and the one that gives us the most control occurs when we "take the bull by the horns" and begin to deal with the conflict directly by initiating a confrontation. When the confrontation is brought on by the situation, results can sometimes be disastrous. Take, for example, a man who knows that he is seriously overweight. He also knows the risks of heart disease as they relate to obesity. He has a habit of eating too much, and too much of the wrong kinds of foods. Every time he reads an article or is given a warning, he feels guilty (distress) for not doing what he knows he should. Every time he sits down to eat, he experiences an intrapersonal conflict between what he knows and what he has conditioned himself to do. Then comes the confrontation. He wakes up one day in a coronary intensive care unit. Unwilling to personally confront the conflict, its feelings and consequent warnings about his relationship with the environment, he has allowed a situation (heart attack) to take away his option of gaining control of the situation, and with disastrous results.

This is an extreme example, but things like this happen regularly.

We are not the only ones who can be expected to confront conflict. Other people who are directly or indirectly involved will exercise their option as well. In addition, third party interventions can also precipitate confrontation. If the skills of the intervening person are good and if she or he engages in conscious management, the outcome can be positive. Unfortunately, when other people confront, they usually apply the bad management habits they have acquired over the years. When this happens, the conflict can rapidly degenerate and movement from one conflict stage to another can occur quickly.

Confrontations mark the spot where resolutions begin. Confrontation represents the most significant opportunity to effectively take charge of a conflict and bring good management to bear on its resolution.

SUMMARY

For most of us, children included, conflict is an unsettling experience that begins with a feeling of confusion or loss of control — feelings of distress. Most of us, in reacting to and dealing with conflict, have developed some very bad habits. A final review of our model helps us to put the nature of conflict in perspective.

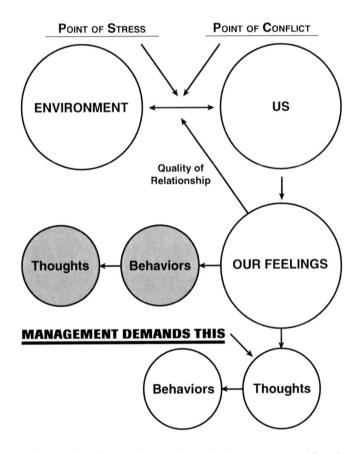

Our model shows the relationship between ourself and our varied environments. In section two, we examined the sources of conflict. All are found in our environment. How we perceive the things in our environment is determined by who we are. All the things we have learned and come to believe combine with our basic human traits to shape our perceptions.

The mechanism that supports this is Mindworks. The Reticular Activating System (RAS) is at the center of an amazing network that links all the operating systems of the brain/mind complex and facilitates the processing of our perceptions as they are turned into physical responses and feelings.

Mindworks —

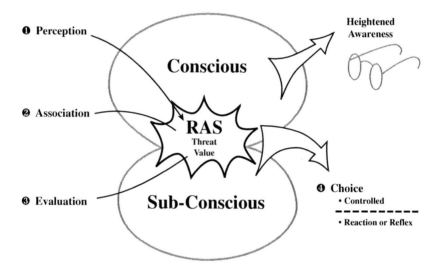

As RAS processes perceptions, those perceptions develop emotional significance and are translated into feelings at the conscious level. Our feelings reflect the quality of the relationship between ourself and our environment. As we experience feelings, one of two things takes place. We either consciously choose to act or we unconsciously react to our feelings. Which we do makes all the difference.

If we react, which is the most common choice, we move from feelings to behavior that is orchestrated on our habits of dealing with conflict (usually less than optimum). The outcome of this initial behavior generates new thoughts that trigger new perceptions and the cycle begins all over again, still without conscious control or the benefit of self-management.

If we choose to act consciously, we move from our feelings to thoughts. Here we can assess the situation and begin making conscious and controlled choices about how to deal with it. Based on our thinking, we can then manage our behaviors in a restrained manner that permits a different cycle to develop. This cycle also creates new perceptions, but continues to be on the conscious plain. It is only in this way that we are able to effectively take charge of conflict. This is the essence of self-management, and conflict management demands self-management first.

Internal and External Conflict.

We experience two kinds of conflict. Internal conflicts occur within an individual when beliefs and desires clash, often during times of decision making or in stress-laden situations. External conflicts are those that involve two or more people. They may be interpersonal (between or among individuals), or intergroup (between various groups of individuals).

Since every conflict engages Mindworks, all conflicts have an internal component. Whereas intrapersonal conflicts are strictly internal, every external conflict is also internal in nature. Because we experience both, we must develop the skills necessary to deal with both effectively.

Whether internal or external, active conflict management begins with effectively confronting the conflict.

5.

TAKING CHARGE OF
ORGANIZATIONAL CONFLICT

5. DIALOGUE HOLDS THE KEY

The word *dialogue* comes from two Greek roots, dia and logos, suggesting "meaning flowing through." Dialogue is the vehicle by which we produce shared meaning. As a discipline, the process of dialogue greatly facilitates collective learning and inquiry by transforming the quality of conversation and the thinking that supports it.

Complex issues, such as those challenging today's organizations, require the intelligence and creativity of many minds, rather than the solutions of a single individual. Yet in the face of difficult problems and conflicts, people often cling to rigid positions, and groups tend to factionalize or completely break down. The result is watered-down compromises and tenuous commitment to goals.

> Complex issues, such as those challenging today's organizations, require the intelligence and creativity of many minds, rather than solutions of a single individual.

By contrast, dialogue doesn't require compromise; it doesn't even require agreement. Instead, it encourages people to participate in a pool of shared meaning. Dialogue is not a problem-solving technique; it is a means of exploration that can lead to enlightened action.

William Isaacs, director of The Dialogue Project, part of the Organizational Learning Center at MIT, has conducted extensive research on dialogue in corporate, political and social settings around the world. Through his work with groups, Isaacs has constructed a model that describes the developmental stages of dialogue.

According to Isaacs' model, dialogue progresses through up to four stages, each involving a developmental crisis. The resolution of the crisis at each stage determines whether a group continues to develop dialogue or slips into conventional discussion and debate.

Stage 1: When people first come together to "dialogue," the initial crisis occurs as participants realize that the situation is far different than the kinds of meetings to which they are accustomed — no leader, agenda, stated task, or required decisions. This in itself causes considerable discomfort. As people begin to converse, they "weigh out" one another's differences and areas of agreement, and explore the range of assumptions present.

Stage 2: During exploration the tendency emerges for individuals to defend their positions on various issues. Conflicts arise between opposing points of view and participants soon realize that, in order to proceed further, they must suspend (not suppress) judgment so that they can listen to others *and* to themselves.

Stage 3: If the majority of the group succeeds in suspending judgment and stays together, the process enters a period of creative inquiry. Participants begin to explore topics and points of view "coolly," without ego identification. In the process, they examine habitual patterns of interaction, realizing how those limit creative inquiry. This leads to a third crisis in which participants experience a degree of pain and despair concerning the isolation and creative limitations that they (and humans in general) impose upon themselves.

Stage 4: Out of this painful awareness comes the final stage of development, which is characterized by the realization that the group, having sufficiently and without judgment explored its divergent views, shares a rich pool of common meaning. Isaacs calls the communication at this stage *metalogue* which means "moving or flowing with." Observations about process blend subtly with content information. The use of narrative as a medium for communication increases, making communication more creative and evocative.

A MEDIUM FOR DIALOGUE

The Group Work Circle, introduced in this text (page 189), offers a contained but highly suitable venue for developing dialogue. The circle process is built on the notion of diversity and of developing pools of shared meaning. If used regularly over an extended period of time, the 20-minute circle accomplishes many of the things Isaacs observes in dialogue groups meeting for several hours a day over a number of days. Participants suspend judgment, listen to divergent points of view, build trust and rapport, and generate ideas and insights in a "cool" atmosphere of mutual respect. Aside from the length of sessions, a major distinction of the Group Work Circle is that initial communication centers around a specific topic, while follow-up discussion can range quite freely.

INCREASING AWARENESS

By participating in the Group Work Circle, individuals have many opportunities to focus on their feelings, thoughts, and behaviors, and those of others. Through regular verbal sharing, they develop an awareness of their feelings, they talk about their responses, and they listen to how others have responded in similar situations. Their ability to evaluate the appropriateness of various behaviors increases.

By verbally exploring their own experiences in the circle and listening to others do the same, participants begin to see each person, including themselves, as unique. Feelings of concern and responsibility develop as the needs, problems, values, and preferences of others penetrate their awareness.

This awareness of the enhancing qualities of diversity is a major ingredient in the productive management of conflict. Differing preferences, positions, and points of view — frequently the seeds of confrontation and conflict — contribute to the "rich pool of common meaning" described by Isaacs as stage-four *metalogue*. And it is all accomplished through dialogue — through *words*.

Words are the only tool we have for systematically turning our attention and awareness to the feelings within us, and for describing and reflecting on our thoughts and behaviors. The effective use of words constitutes the first step in developing the ability to grasp previously unspoken feelings and understand the connection between feelings and behavior, including behaviors that precipitate conflict. With practice, individuals become more and more adept at making these connections. This knowledge in turn develops the capacity to evaluate alternatives and to think before and during actions.

ACHIEVING MASTERY

In addition to increasing awareness, the dialogue that occurs in the Group Work Circle can contribute immensely to achieving mastery of that brief cognitive moment that invariably precedes conflict — that instant on the threshold of conflict before the cognitive mind is engulfed by pre-programmed and often unproductive responses from the emotional mind. Achieving mastery implies not only recognizing and extending the cognitive moment, but enjoying the self-confidence that comes with knowing that any situation, no matter how volatile, can be consciously managed.

Through participation in Group Work Circles, individuals systematically explore their successes and failures in dealing with conflict. Circle topics can be selected specifically to heighten awareness of the range of conflict behaviors represented in the group. In this context, successes and failures become realities to be examined. The objective is not to lavish praise on some participants while reminding others they have failed; instead, the circle process enables participants to see that success and failure (and everything in between) are common and universal and are experienced by all people when they strive to accomplish things. Thus, a wide range of meaning is allowed to flow through the circle process.

Circle topics may address human relations competencies as well. Topics related to including others, assuming and sharing responsibility, offering help, behaving assertively, and solving problems all bear directly or indirectly on the issue of conflict. In addition, the circle is a wonderful tool for encouraging cooperation. As equitably as possible, the circle structure attempts to meet the needs of all participants. Everyone's feelings are accepted. Judgments are suspended. The circle is not another competitive arena, but is guided by a spirit of collaboration. When participants practice fair, respectful interaction with one another, they benefit from the experience and are likely to employ these responsible behaviors in other work (and personal) situations.

Finally, the circle enables participants to expand their repertoire of conflict strategies. Through the narrative sharing of experiences, participants hear many examples of specific tactics and strategies applied in a variety of conflict situations. Through discussion (following the sharing phase of the circle) the range of alternative behaviors receives further exploration and examination.

DEVELOPING INTERPERSONAL SKILLS

The need to promote positive, effective interpersonal relations is a challenge faced by all organizations. To the degree that organizations are social institutions, encouraging members or employees to coexist peacefully and to interact flexibly, skillfully, and responsibly, becomes an inescapable mandate.

Healthy working relationships are built upon positive interpersonal experiences between colleagues; however, organizations generally have no systematic way of helping employees to understand and get along with each other. The Group Work Circle provides both system and setting.

Circles are marvelous testing grounds where people can observe themselves and others in action, and can begin to see

> Healthy working
> realtionships are
> built upon positive
> interpersonal
> experiences
> between and
> among colleagues.

themselves as contributing to the feelings and performance of others. With this understanding, individuals are helped to conclude that being responsible towards others feels good and is the most valuable and rewarding form of interaction. These attitudes benefit not only conflict prevention, but the productive resolution of conflict when it occurs.

In addition, the ability to make accurate interpretations and responses in interpersonal situations contributes to a broad and practical sense of organizational values or ethics. When people possess this ability, they know where they stand with themselves and others. They can tell what actions "fit" a situation, and are aware of not only how others affect them, but how their actions affect their colleagues and the organizational culture as a whole.

LISTENING — THE MASTER SKILL

Of all the interpersonal skills, the most important is listening. The willingness and ability of one person to attend to, process, and understand the verbal and/or nonverbal messages of another human being is what makes communication possible. Messages can be sent in many ways — we can speak, sing, yell, cry, shout, and indulge in an endless variety of gestures, postures, and facial expressions — but if no one is listening, if no one is paying attention, communication simply does not occur.

> Of all the conflict
> management skills,
> the most important
> is also listening.

Arguably, of all the conflict management skills, the most important is also listening. Why? Because listening demonstrates respect, which instantly diffuses conflict. Because listening says, "You are important." "Your concerns are important." "Your opinion is valued." And because listening builds trust and helps parties disengage from high-profile conflict positions.

Listening is also the premier skill of third party mediators and of the people to whom we gravitate for help when we have a problem. Unfortunately, some of the people to whom we would *like* to talk turn out to be poor choices because they don't know *how* to listen. They have the mistaken notion that when we describe a problem, we're asking them for a solution. Before we've even explained the problem, they're out rounding up a posse or forming a lynching party. They've jumped to conclusions and quickly diagnosed our problem, and they're usually wrong. If they'd just listen awhile, they might learn what is really troubling us. Listeners learn, while talkers reveal how much they've failed to learn about communication.

LISTENING IS SITUATIONAL

Depending on our objectives, we tend to listen in different ways. For example:

• **Appreciative** listening is what we do when our favorite music is playing. In this type of situation, listening gives us pleasure and satisfaction.

• **Discriminative** listening is what we do when we attune our senses to identify the source of a sound in the next room or on the street outside, or attempt to identify a person based on voice alone.

At times like these, listening becomes more acute and we focus all our energy into this one sensory device. Think about it: How do your mind and body react when you hear a sound in the dark?

TRY THIS!

"Hum Dinger"

Pick three or four familiar songs, such as "Row, Row, Row Your Boat," "The Star Spangled Banner," and

"Oh Susanna!" Write the titles on separate slips of paper, repeating each title as many times as necessary to ensure that every person gets a title. (For example: 3 titles X 5 copies/each supplies a group of 15 participants.) Next, distribute the titles, announcing that there will be *no talking* during the exercise. Instruct participants to begin humming their tune as soon as they receive their slip of paper. Tell them to move about the room listening to the tunes of other people, and to form a team with other folks who are humming the same tune. This is an enjoyable way to form circle groups or other team formations.

• **Comprehensive** listening is engaged in for the purpose of gathering data. Usually the information has value for some future use, such as planning, writing, studying, or reporting to others. Listening for the purpose of data gathering requires considerable energy and concentration because accuracy is usually of prime importance.

TRY THIS!

Group Work (See page 189)

To help people become more aware of their own listening behaviors, use the topic, "A Time I Should Have Listened More Carefully."

Here's an idea for elaborating —

Recall a time when you made a mistake, or couldn't find your destination, or failed to do something important — simply because you didn't listen. Describe the situation and the consequences of your lapse in listening behavior.

After everyone who would like to share has had an opportunity, facilitate a discussion with the following question (record responses on a sheet of paper):

—*What can you do to improve the accuracy of your listening today?*

Conclude by summarizing techniques for improving listening ability.

• **Critical** listening is done with the intent to pass judgment. For example, a professor participating in the oral examination of a graduate student must listen critically in order to assess the student's knowledge and skills. A supervisor listening to a work group describe its findings relative to a crucial project will not be able to reinforce or redirect the group unless critical listening is applied. The danger with critical listening is that used inappropriately (when someone simply wants to talk, for instance) it can be a strong deterrent to communication.

• **Therapeutic** listening is the most neutral of all listening forms. It is the mainstay of helping relationships, the number one skill of counselors, psychologists, and psychiatrists. Therapeutic listeners demonstrate empathy, reflect feelings, and use feedback and skillful questioning to guide people through problem solving.

TRY THIS!

Group Work (See page 189)

To help people recognize the relevance of listening to their own lives, use the topic, "A Time Someone Should Have Listened to Me, But Didn't."

Here's an idea for elaborating —

Think of a time when you had something important to

say — a crucial piece of information to share or strong feelings that you wanted to convey. However, the person to whom you were attempting to talk didn't listen, or pretended to listen but obviously didn't get the message. What happened as a result of this person's failure to listen?

After everyone who would like to has had a chance to share, facilitate a discussion with the following question (record responses on a sheet of paper):

—How did you feel when you weren't listened to?

Conclude with a general discussion concerning the importance of listening.

BARRIERS TO LISTENING

Effective listening is a skill. Like any other skill, competency in listening is achieved through learning and practice. Conscious repetition, feedback and correction of specific behaviors associated with listening leads to a gradual mastery of this "master" skill.

> A mind constantly buzzing with plans, daydreams, schemes and anxieties is difficult to clear, and good listening requires the temporary suspension of all unrelated thoughts.

Unfortunately, the scarcity of good listeners is self-perpetuating; without good listeners to learn from and (especially) models to emulate, we simply do not learn this skill. Instead, we learn whatever passes for listening in our environment: distracted half-attention, constant interruptions, multi-layered, high-volume, talk-fest free-for-alls with no listening at all.

Even after acquiring a modicum of listening ability, we still face many barriers that inhibit or prevent us from giving our full attention to the thoughts and feelings of others. Perceived lack of time is the first and most common barrier. A life programmed with back-to-back commitments offers little leeway for listening. Similarly, a mind constantly buzzing with plans, daydreams, schemes and anxieties is difficult to clear, and good listening requires the temporary suspension of all unrelated thoughts — a blank canvas. In order to become effective listeners, we have to learn to manage what goes on in our own minds.

Technology, for all its glorious gifts, has also erected substantial barriers to listening. Face-to-face meetings and telephone conversations (priceless listening opportunities) are being replaced by E-mail and the sterile anonymity of electronic meeting rooms. Meanwhile television continues to capture countless hours that might otherwise be available for conversation, dialogue, and listening.

Distress is a common barrier, too. The willingness and ability to listen are easily extinguished by worry, fear, anger, grief, and numerous other responses from the emotional mind.

TRY THIS!

Touch the thumb of one hand to the forefinger of the same hand, making the sign variously interpreted as "right on!" "perfect!" or "got it!" Ask participants to make the same sign. Now begin to describe (verbally) where you want participants to place the finger sign, at the same time demonstrating each movement. For example: "Put it on top of your head," "Look through it like a lens," "Put it over your third finger like a ring," and "Run it up and down your forearm." Once into the pattern, say "Put it next to your cheek," but instead of demonstrating your words, model placing the finger sign against your chin. Watch to see how many people mimic your action, without regard for the contradictory words. Use this exercise to highlight the importance of eyes as well as ears in listening, and to underscore the fact that verbal and nonverbal cues don't always match. It is important to pay attention to both.

TRY THIS!

Briefly discuss with participants the importance of eye contact during conversation. Ask them to help you create a situation that will give them an opportunity experience the effects of eye contact.

Have participants sit facing a partner. Instruct the partners to decide who is A and who is B. Instruct A to talk to B for 1 minute about the topic, "What I Like About My Favorite Sport or Hobby." Instruct B to listen, but *not to look* at A. B can look at the floor, ceiling, out the window, or anywhere except at A. After 1 minute, call time and allow A to share his/her feelings and reactions with B for another minute.

Repeat the entire exercise, only this time instruct B to look (not stare) directly into A's eyes, maintaining good eye contact. Allow 1 minute for the exercise and 1 minute for sharing reactions.

Finally have the partners switch roles and repeat both parts of the exercise, with B the speaker and A the listener. You might want to suggest a new topic, such as "Something I'm Looking Forward to This Weekend."

Debrief the exercise with the entire group. Emphasize that eye contact is but one important dimension of body language. If time allows, ask the group to brainstorm other dimensions.

LISTENING OUT LOUD

As good listeners, we are not merely silent receptacles, passively receiving the thoughts and feelings of others. We respond with verbal and nonverbal cues which let the speaker know — actually *prove* — that we are listening and understanding. These responses are called *feedback*.

Verbal feedback works best when delivered in the form of brief statements, rather than questions. (Our questions usually get answered if we wait.) Statements allow us to paraphrase and reflect what we've heard, which affirms the speaker's success at communicating and encourages the speaker to elaborate further or delve more deeply into the topic. Meaningful exchanges are built on feedback.

In order to accurately feed back a person's thoughts and feelings, we have to be consciously, actively engaged in the process of listening. Hearing a statement, we create a mental model, vicariously experiencing what the speaker is describing, feeling the speaker's feelings through the filters of our own humanity and experience.

As good listeners, our *nonverbal* feedback is equally in tune with the speaker. An occasional nod of the head, attentive posture, and leaning *toward* the speaker demonstrate interest; facial expressions change appropriately to show that we share the speaker's concern, doubt, anger, amusement, happiness, worry, and other emotions. These behaviors occur naturally when we are *really* listening with conscious, active engagement.

CONFLICT CONNECTION

One of the approaches this book strongly suggests for managing confrontations is "Prepare a Place and Make It Holy" (page 117). A primary reason for seeking a safe, relaxed environment during confrontations and conflicts is so that we can listen effectively. Listening is a pre-eminent method by which we absorb negative energy in confrontational and crisis situations. Listening diffuses emotional powder kegs and allows people to let off steam.

MORE BENEFITS OF LISTENING

One of the principle benefits of listening is that it produces *more* listening. Good listeners are models. Consciously and unconsciously, we emulate their behaviors.

By listening, we demonstrate the value we have for the person who is speaking. Listening is a gift of time — one of the most precious commodities we have.

Listening is efficient. It promotes clarity, accuracy, and understanding and thereby helps us achieve quality, excellence and (within the organization) lower costs.

Listening promotes learning — the sharing of knowledge, expertise, insight, and intelligence.

Listening builds trust. When we listen without judgment we communicate openness and exhibit a spaciousness that says, "All of you fits comfortably here. Be who you are. I can deal with it." When people realize that they don't have to disguise or withhold parts of themselves in order to have our respect, they relax, they feel safe, and they begin to trust us.

TAKING CHARGE OF
ORGANIZATIONAL CONFLICT

6. MANAGING CONFRONTATIONS

Confronting a conflict is the initial step toward its resolution.

Until a conflict is confronted, the level of distress experienced by the parties involved usually increases as they anticipate finally having to face up to the situation.

Confronting a conflict is not to be confused with a common form of conflict called a "confrontation". Think of it this way: Confronting is a *verb* while a confrontation is a *noun*. A simple but important distinction.

Conflict management differs from confrontation management. Through effective management, a conflict can be escalated, de-escalated, or brought to resolution. Confrontation is an important step in the resolution process. Much of the quality of the rest of the resolution effort depends on how well we handle the initial confrontation. A single conflict may require a number of confrontations before it is finally resolved because a conflict generated by one issue frequently produces other issues which, in turn, must be dealt with. Consider this situation:

An experienced and valued supervisor is removed by top managers from her position as the head of an important interdepartmental committee. The confrontation occurs without warning, and the supervisor reacts as though a land mine has exploded under her accomplishments, her plans, and her self-esteem. Whatever conflict existed over the supervisor's committee leadership and the goals of top managers is now complicated by a more volatile conflict regarding how the deed was carried out. The supervisor is vocal in her outrage. Her colleagues choose sides and polarize. The supervisor calls in sick and threatens to file a grievance. The productivity of her entire department is negatively affected.

~~Sometimes we have a chance to prepare for confrontations,~~
but often (as in the case of the supervisor in the example
above) they seem to drop on us right out of the sky when we
are least prepared and there is little time to consider our
options. When we are caught off guard, we must be ready
with some basic understanding of the nature and dynamics of
conflict in general and some easy-to-use approaches to handling confrontations specifically.

In discussing the distinction between styles of managing
conflict and strategies for managing conflict, we learned that
styles are automatic responses. They manifest themselves
throughout the conflict, but can have the greatest impact,
particularly on interpersonal conflicts, at the point of confrontation.

TRY THIS!

Here's a small group activity that will assist people in
identifying the ways they tend to approach
confrontations. Write one of the following conflict
situations on each of six index cards or half-sheets of
paper.

1. You've just confronted your son/daughter
concerning several issues. Your first concern is the
late hours your child is keeping (staying out late or just
watching TV). Next, you don't approve of the friends
with whom your child is associating. Finally (and
you're convinced the hours and friends have
something to do with this), you are upset about your
child's failure to finish homework and about concerns
expressed by teachers. Your son/daughter totally
disagrees with your position.

2. One of the things you take great pride in is your
punctuality. Unfortunately, your spouse makes you
crazy by always being a little (or a lot) late. That's
okay except when it makes you late. And even that's

okay except for those occasions when it's really important for you to be on time. You and your spouse have been asked by your new boss to come to her home for dinner. Everything is on schedule and you're all ready to leave with plenty of time to spare, when you discover that your spouse isn't going to be ready for another half hour. This is going to make you late. What's more, if you leave on time, you beat rush hour traffic and now you'll be in the middle of it, which will slow you down further. This is the last straw, and you're going to make your upset known, but your spouse just says, "Well, what do you want me to do?"

3. Your son borrowed $30.00 from you on the condition that he pay you back by washing your car every Saturday morning for six weeks. You agreed, but now three weeks have gone by and you're upset that the car hasn't been washed once. You wonder why you have waited so long to speak with your son seriously about this, but now, when you do, he says you're asking too much.

4. You purchased a new sofa from a furniture manufacturer and made a 20% down payment with your order. You were promised that the sofa would be ready for you in three weeks. Now, almost six weeks after you placed your order, you've taken delivery only to find that the workmanship is terrible. You are totally dissatisfied. When you telephone, the manufacturer tells you that the only thing the company can offer you in return for your new sofa is a credit against another purchase less a twenty percent return charge. You are livid and are now standing in the manager's office ready to do battle.

5. It's Friday afternoon, and you've had a terrible week. You're standing in line at the bank waiting to make a deposit and get cash for the weekend. Just when you find yourself next in line, someone walks in front of you and approaches the next open teller who

promptly begins to wait on this person. Knowing you were next in line, you're justifiably upset and start to boil. At that moment the bank manager approaches and asks you if everything is all right.

6. It's been a hectic week out of town, and now you've just settled into your seat on the plane for the long flight home. Just as you start relaxing, another passenger appears and tells you she's been assigned the seat in which you are sitting. You check your ticket envelope and confirm that you've both been assigned the same seat. The other passenger indicates that she is just as anxious to get home as you are. The passenger service representative for the airline explains that the flight is oversold, no one else wants to give up a seat, and one of you will have to wait until the next day to fly home.

Have people form groups of six to eight. Provide each group with a different situation. Introduce the activity by explaining that everyone handles conflict situations a little differently. Have the participants discuss within their groups what they'd do in the situation, and have each person explain how she or he would handle it.

Ask each group to select a recorder to note the suggested approaches and be prepared to share a couple of them with the larger group. There are no right or wrong answers; people should share what they would most likely do.

Acknowledge that each person has approaches that work better than others, and that sometimes people wish they'd done things differently. Facilitate a discussion by asking the following question:

— *Why is it that we sometimes do things in confrontive situations we later regret or wish we'd done differently? (Answers should include some reference to habitual behaviors.)*

It's difficult to change these conditioned responses, however much can be done in the short term to improve our ability to respond to confrontations. If engaged in consciously and consistently, these approaches can help us form new habits over the long term.

> **Rule of Objectivity —**
> It is essential to elevate oneself above the plane of emotional content in order to manage a confrontation. We must focus on the object of the confrontation (objectivity) and not on the subjects involved in it.

It's very important to know what we want to accomplish during a confrontation. Since the parties involved in a confrontation are likely to bring to it high levels of negative emotional energy, the first thing to do is begin disarming and diffusing this energy. This helps prevent the conflict from escalating and allows the parties to start looking at it objectively.

It's critical to keep the focus on the problem or issue and not on the parties to the conflict.

Once we are able to contain the emotional content of the conflict, we can then move to defining the problem. This step helps us contain the conflict and reduces the likelihood that it will expand to other issues or areas. The more we can contain the conflict, the more manageable it becomes and the fewer resources it consumes.

When we have diffused its emotional content and contained the conflict by defining its source, we have established control and can move ahead with strategic management activities.

All this sounds quite simple, but when we start adding people to the picture it quickly becomes very complex. Every party to the conflict is bringing his or her own diversity to it. This multitude of perceptions makes the process of managing a conflict very difficult. Unless control is established early, most conflicts get out of hand quickly and the energy and resources needed to establish control at some later point seem to increase exponentially.

Given the importance of confrontation as an opportunity to establish early control over a conflict situation, it's vital to have ready a number of easy to use approaches that can be quickly employed.

Remember that all you want to accomplish in the confrontation is to diffuse the emotional energy, to elevate the conflict to a conscious plane, to contain its spread, and reduce the chances of it escalating.

An important rule to keep in mind is to confront the conflict as early as possible. The longer you wait the more energy builds and the more debilitating the conflict becomes.

FIRST AID FAST

The intent of managing confrontations is to stabilize the situation and restore balance and equilibrium long enough to permit application of long-term solutions and remedies. It's a lot like rendering first aid.

The following tools can be used to take control of confrontations and restore balance long enough for individuals to begin engaging in more strategic approaches and problem solving. Let's look first at interpersonal conflicts and then come back to intrapersonal.

Most confrontations have immediate potential for becoming higher-level conflicts. Very often, little or no time is available to consider a wide range of management and resolution strategies. This section provides quick access to the tools you will want to have at hand when a confrontation occurs. Keep these tools readily available to refer to in preparation for an anticipated confrontation. Review them alone, or with your staff, as a means of maintaining a high level of readiness so that when you are called on to respond in a confrontive situation — even a surprise confrontation — you will be as prepared as possible. Use them as a foundation on which to build an arsenal of tools for disarming and diffusing difficult situations so that they can be contained, controlled, managed, and ultimately resolved.

Expect Expectations —

Most people engaging in confrontation do so with preconceptions or expectations. Anticipating and understanding these expectations provides an excellent place to begin diffusing and disarming a confrontation.

A common view held by those people anticipating conflict is, "Expect the worst and hope for the best..." The other part of this statement is usually, "...that way you'll never be disappointed." Avoid this mindset, as it holds little promise for producing positive results. Instead, ask two questions so that you can understand the range of possible outcomes:

1. What would I like to have happen?
2. What do I expect to happen, or what do I think is going to happen?

NOTE THE CONTRAST: The first question sets up the best outcome you can hope for, while the second question is likely to give you the worst-case scenario.

Put Them First —

Most of the time when a confrontation arises, we are occupied with other tasks. The natural temptation is to subordinate the conflict to the task at hand. Don't! Put the person or persons you're dealing with in any confrontation in a priority position. This is crucial!

> Always make it clear that people and their problems are number one.

Always make it clear that people and their problems are number one.

Never interrupt, even when you have something constructive to say or find yourself in agreement. If you do, you will be seen as argumentative and that can only deepen the problem or add a new one that might sound like this:

"I went in to talk about my assignment with the boss and all I got was an argument."

Don't let either people or things distract you, and if the confrontation is taking place over the telephone, never put the person on hold or delay your response to him or her. The best motto for phone situations is . . .

GET THE FACTS AND GET BACK.

Other ways to "Put Them First" include using the next two tools in combination:

Prepare a Place and Make It Holy

2. Are You Listening?

WARNING! Never use acronyms or jargon unless you are certain the other parties to the confrontation understand their meaning. They almost always intimidate, confuse, and insult.

Prepare a Place and Make It Holy —

Among the easiest things you can do is to prepare a place in which to accommodate confrontive situations. The impact of a relaxed, peaceful, safe place is frequently all that is needed to disarm a difficult situation. Every floor or department needs a trauma center.

TRY THIS!

Starting with *relaxing, peaceful* and *safe*, ask participants to brainstorm with you the qualities or characteristics that could be used to describe an environment that is perfect for disarming and diffusing confrontational situations. Include physical things like music, plants, etc.

On a chalkboard or piece of chart paper, record brainstormed items until you have a long list.

Now start a discussion by reviewing the list and asking participants the following questions:

— *Do you think an investment in a place like this would produce commensurate payoffs when it comes to managing confrontations? What would the payoffs be?*

If you are dealing with people from outside the organization, here are some things that should *not* be in this special environment:

Awards

News clippings

Certificates

A mess

Be professional but not braggadocios!

Are You Listening?

Because of the emotional nature of confrontations, first-aid listening requires conscious awareness and control. Here are the tips you can use to restore equilibrium to a confrontive situation.

Listen first for feelings and then for facts.

This is critical. Don't just listen to the feelings of the other person, listen to your own as well. Feelings are the key indicators of what's going on in a situation and for each of the individuals involved. Pay attention to these important clues. When you do, you will find it easier to maintain conscious control of your own emotional state.

Don't interrupt even if you have a solution or are in agreement. Just let people get whatever is bothering them "off their chest."

Don't even break in for clarification. Just be patient and wait. This permits venting. Venting has a cathartic effect and accomplishes two things. Venting allows the release of pent-up energy, and it gives you a chance to restore control.

VERY IMPORTANT! Never take exception with what's being said AND, if at all possible, avoid using the word "BUT." It's a killer because it means you are arguing.

Move From Right to Left —

The emotional aspect of a conflict is a right-brain phenomenon while the objective aspects are all left brain. By getting parties to focus on the problem rather than on their emotions, you are able to apply the rule of objectivity, keep the conflict from becoming personal, and elevate it to a conscious and manageable level.

Taking the wind out of the emotional side of a confrontation lets you begin to focus on the more substantive issues, whether they involve tangible things or personal values.

Here are a couple of rules to keep in mind:

1. Don't usurp the feelings of the other person. It's okay to say, "I understand how you feel." Never add, "I'd feel the same way." The second phrase only justifies the person's upset and keeps him or her in an emotional state.

2. Focus on the facts. Ask a left-brain question to get the focus off the emotional content and on to the situation. For example, ask about when the incident took place, or who was involved. Who, what, where, when, and how questions are useful. Don't ever ask "why" questions. They call for speculation and tend to heighten emotions. Remember the Rule of Objectivity: It is essential to elevate oneself above the plane of emotional content in order to manage confrontation.

Absorbing Energy —

Aside from the conscious tools we can employ to diffuse and disarm confrontation, there are a number of behaviors that we can exhibit in confrontive situations that go far to absorb the high levels of energy people bring to these situations.

When energy is running high, add an extra measure of self-management to a situation.

Here are some things you can try:

1. Use a soft, low voice when speaking.

2. Be conscious of your pace both in speaking and moving — slow it down.

3. Keep an open posture and remove obstacles like desks and tables.
4. Make appropriate eye contact. (Avoiding eye contact in tense situations says we're intimidated and lack control.)
5. Provide well-paced and thoughtful responses (avoid humor).
6. Make the other person right until you know otherwise.

TRY THIS!

Most people can identify simple techniques they have learned to use that have value in disarming and containing a confrontation. After reviewing the list above, have people take a moment and think of any other approaches they have found useful.

Ask the group to share these and create a list on the chalkboard or chart paper.

Ask the following question to bring closure:

— *What part of our behavior in a confrontation helps us take charge?*

Getting to Want —

Whatever obvious things people want from confrontive encounters, or no matter how much altruism or objectivity is evident in their arguments, be assured that everyone is operating from some level of self-interest. "Wants" are directly tied to the source of the conflict and are the real objects of resolution. Accumulated wants are primary motivators in confrontation. Understanding and clarifying wants is vital to achieving desirable outcomes.

We are more motivated by wants than needs.

Many people enter conflict without a clear idea of just

> We are more motivated by wants than needs.

what it is they want. Using this tool can de-escalate a conflict and put it into the realm of a resolvable problem where the objective is to present alternatives among which a want can be defined.

By helping people clarify their wants, we engage *their* self-interest and move from being perceived as an adversary to being perceived as an ally.

What Can I Do?

This is perhaps the most important question you can ask. It slices to the issues by approaching them from the results end rather than focusing on causes or blame. Use this as a possible first response after you've just listened.

Most of the time the individual(s) won't have a clear idea of what possibilities or constraints exist. (Some problems have no solutions, or are beyond our control.) By asking this question, you give the person a further opportunity to clarify desires, and you also provide an opening for the person to take charge of the situation by providing a range of possibilities.

REMEMBER — Your job at this point is to reestablish balance and equilibrium to the situation. After this, you can move to creating a resolution.

What I Will Do —

By offering to take immediate and clear actions aimed at the concerns of those involved in the confrontation, you begin the discovery process that leads to resolution.

Sometimes a course of action is obvious, and you can be specific as to how you plan to go about resolving the problem. Always remember that the more agreement you can get from the other person regarding this course of action, the farther you move toward resolving the problem.

Even if you are just going to gather other information, make clear that you ARE GOING TO DO SOMETHING. Also be clear as to WHEN YOU'RE GOING TO DO IT, and finally, see to it that IT'S DONE.

Mea Culpa —

Though it sounds easy, most of us find it difficult to apologize. "I'm sorry" is a simple phrase, yet a powerful means of setting the stage for meaningful discussion of problems and issues. It lets others know you are assuming a measure of responsibility in bringing about a solution or resolution.

On occasion, a mistake is made that needs to be admitted openly. With such an admission you need to be sure to detail what actions have been taken, or will be taken, to ensure that the problem doesn't develop again.

A twist on "Mea Culpa" is to use it as a way of disarming a volatile situation by saying, "I'm sorry this has happened (no admission of guilt), and I'll do whatever it takes to get it resolved."

Neutralize and Reduce Resistance —

Here are some specific things you can do to break through resistance that exists when people are emotionally attached either to an issue or an expectation. This is how to create alignment around the management and ultimate resolution of conflicts.

Many people enter confrontation and conflict "locked on" to particular beliefs and values. The way they see it, the issue reflects on their beliefs. When they perceive insensitivity to what they believe in, a strong resistance to change develops.

To counteract this, it is important to discover what values and beliefs are driving the situation. This is best done by asking for opinions or feelings about the problem that is at the heart of the confrontation or conflict.

Very often, what appears to be the obvious cause, masks a deeper concern. For example, people may say that they don't like a new approach that has been suggested, and they don't think it will work and therefore cannot give it their support. On the surface the new approach may seem like the problem, but when care is given to listening and seeking clarification, the problem may prove to be that the people are afraid that they won't be able to perform in the new situation and don't want to be seen as possibly lacking ability. The fear, rather than the approach is the source of the conflict. Until you are able to address this concern, long-term resolution is impossible.

In confrontive situations, where resolution is not the primary aim, much is accomplished by simply acknowledging that another point of view exists. By making room for whatever values and/or beliefs are being brought to the situation, you are able to restore comfort, reduce and neutralize resistance, an create balance and equilibrium.

Do Your Homework —

Not only is this an outstanding prevention tool, it is a great way to determine the extent of a problem. Very often, we only see the tip of the iceberg when facing a confrontation. When the confrontation articulates a symptom of a greater problem, this tool allows us to get to the cause.

Two interesting rules apply here:

1. The 1 to 27 Rule — Only one person in twenty-seven will ultimately complain to you about his or her problem.

2. The 9 to 25 Rule — An unhappy or confrontive person will complain to between nine and twenty-five others about his or her problem.

Prior to facing a confrontation — or the first moment that you do — take action to arrest problems before they reach conflict. If you cannot arrest the conflict, contain it. Here's how:

1. Create Forums — settings where individuals and groups feel safe to disclose their concerns and problems. Forums require high trust and must be constantly nurtured. They provide the highest quality input and feedback.

2. Don't wait for a complaint — go fishing! Create mechanisms that genuinely and sincerely solicit information that can help you detect a problem in its early stages, long before it turns into anything but a simple stage-one conflict. Constantly be casting around trying to detect opportunities to capitalize on the potential that lies in each emerging conflict. This approach greatly reduces the number of surprise confrontations. "An ounce of prevention is better than a pound of cure."

3. Create a "local majority" — this concept calls for building a constituency before a problem ever arises. By having a support group in place, you, your work group, or the entire organization can greatly reduce the risk of finding itself having to go on the defensive in a confrontation. This support group will insulate you in confrontations and provide important feedback relative to the potential for conflict.

> If doing your homework sounds like opening a Pandora's Box, remember, if you don't open it, someone else will.

Time spent here is preventative homework, and if doing your homework sounds like opening a Pandora's Box, REMEMBER THIS, if you don't open it, someone else is going to. It's only a matter of time.

Don't Be Part of the Problem —

What we bring to a confrontation or conflict always has some effect . . . make sure it's positive.

HERE ARE SOME CRITICAL THINGS TO REMEMBER ABOUT A CONFRONTATION:

1. Don't ignore it — it won't go away.

2. Don't push it down — sometimes delegation looks like dereliction.

3. No tardy responses — tardiness makes the initial problem bigger and can add a new one.

> When it comes to confrontation, a safe rule is to say the least and do the most.

4. Never argue — the price for needing to be right can be huge.

5. Never guess at the problem — get the facts. Don't solve your problem . . . solve their problem.

When it comes to confrontation, a safe rule is to say less and do more.

Looking Back —

We use many of these tools naturally, but none of us is as good at dealing successfully with confrontations as we could be. In an organizational context, ensuring that a significant number of people possess these abilities almost guaranties a reduction in both numbers and severity of conflicts.

These tools may sound simple; however, keep in mind that they are competing with less effective and even destructive conditioned responses that have been developing over years of practice.

Simply having a knowledge of these tools doesn't do much good. Without practice they are little more than good ideas or intentions. Our habits of response in confrontations have taken years to develop. It is naive to think that just knowing about a better way, and not practicing it, will make much difference.

FIRST AID FOR INTRAPERSONAL CONFLICT

Even personal conflict must be confronted before the resolution process can begin. The same rules and tools that apply to interpersonal confrontations apply to dealing effectively with internal, or intrapersonal, problems. Until confronted, intrapersonal conflicts diminish the ability to perform. Sometimes we repress conflicts, or deny their existence. However, before an intrapersonal problem or conflict reaches such an extreme, it is usually manageable, and getting control of it early is the key to maintaining its manageability.

Recalling the rule of objectivity, remember to keep your attention and focus on the object or cause of the conflict. When you start blaming yourself, you reduce the situation to one of self-recrimination. When this happens, you are no longer in conscious control of the situation, and your conflict can begin to escalate.

The key to maintaining control is to listen to your feelings and respond to them in constructive and thoughtful ways.

SPECIAL CONFRONTATIONS

In the case of certain common situations that we confront almost daily, a few specific strategies have proven useful in maintaining or reestablishing control. Being better able to handle these situations better not only enhances our ability to perform, but also greatly improves the quality of our relationships and our lives.

Managing Criticism —

We are often either recipients of criticism or wish to convey criticism to others. Although loaded with negative connotations, criticism at its best is a means of supplying important feedback and coaching. (You'll find a very useful approach to providing positive and descriptive feedback in section 9. Use it to refine strategic communications related to helping others learn and improve performance.)

Criticism almost always evokes an emotional response from the recipient, and usually produces some level of distress for the individual doing the criticizing.

Here are some simple steps to follow when you are being criticized;

1. Buy yourself some time, and . . .

2. If the criticism is accurate, agree.

3. If you're unsure, ask for specifics and clarification.

4. If you feel the criticism is not accurate, then restate and reaffirm your position or perception until it is acknowledged.

This approach allows you to maintain conscious control over the situation while you objectively evaluate the criticism. There is one practical caveat, however, and that has to do with the power relationship between the person giving the criticism and the person receiving it. If the power disparity is great, then step three becomes extremely important. First, it serves to acknowledge the relationship and the status of the individual giving the criticism. Second, it demonstrates the recipient's ability to successfully engineer a resolution to what will always be perceived as a difficult situation. In this way, the recipient is seen as a person who is easy to get along with and aligned with the interests of the person providing the criticism.

Always remember that in confrontation the objective is to restore stability more than it is to generate resolution.

Managing Anger —

Anger is one of the most common emotions. Anger tells us a lot about the situation we're in or thinking about. Keep in mind that anger is usually a secondary response spawned by some other primary emotion like fear, embarrassment or jealousy. Nevertheless, when we experience the feelings of anger, we need to respond in a controlled manner (usually easier said than done). Remember that anger is a conditioned response, as is the behavior through which we express the anger, unless we deliberately break from what we have been conditioned to do. If we choose to take charge of the situation, here are some simple steps we can follow to establish and maintain control:

1. Buy yourself some time, and . . .

2. Ask yourself these questions:

    a. Is this situation in any way similar to an experience from my past that was emotionally charged?

    b. What other things are going on in my life that might be influencing this anger?

    c. How important is my relationship to this person? . . What is my level of commitment?

    d. What is at risk in this situation?

This approach draws our focus toward the objective aspects of the confrontation and away from the emotional. Similar situations from our past tend to compound the emotional intensity of the current situation as we identify with old feelings. Remember that the perception-association-evaluation process engaged in by the reticular is scanning all of our related past experiences.

Sometimes an unrelated conflict has caused us to be angry and that anger carries over into the situation we are currently confronting. For example, the residue of anger left by an early-morning quarrel at home may be displaced at work on the first person who expresses an opinion contrary to our own. Upset from the other situation can compound the anger experienced in subsequent encounters. As long as we're able to see these feelings as messages about the relationship we're having with our environment, we are able to maintain control.

Very often, we get angry at people or situations that have no real importance to us other than that they violate our need to be right. How often do we get upset at the driver of another car. We don't even know the driver, the driver hasn't hurt us, and yet we waste our energy and lose control of our feelings for no justifiable reason save that we have conditioned ourselves to respond this way.

The last question has to do with safety. It is always important to assess what is at risk in a situation. Remember that in angry confrontations, the level of each person's emotional intensity is different. In situations like these it's important to know the level at which each person is operating. If one party is in stage two and getting more emotionally involved, the risk can be considerable. Keeping in mind that the purpose of a planned confrontation is to establish control of the conflict, we may decide to abandon the confrontation and approach it again when that goal is more achievable and the stakes are not so high.

Remember, too, that if nothing is at risk in the confrontation, there may be no reason to get upset about in the first place. As with the driver whose actions annoy us but do not appreciably affect us, we waste energy being upset when nothing is at risk. A good rule is: the greater the risk, the greater the care with which we approach the confrontation.

Managing moods —

Every confrontation is an emotional experience. Any situation having emotional content produces a chemical imbalance that we experience consciously through feelings and associated physical responses. The chemicals enter our blood stream very quickly, but it takes some time for them to naturally dissipate. Even after the event that produces them has ended, the chemicals remain, and we continue to experience the feelings they produce. We refer to these as residual feelings as moods.

> Remembered or imagined experiences can create the same flood of chemistry as the experience itself. Thinking about a stressful situation produces the same bodily and mental responses as experiencing it.

Whatever our mood, it is the result of the process of perception, association, and evaluation introduced when we addressed the nature of conflict. Good moods are related to positive emotional experiences, while bad moods are related to those that are judged by the subconscious to be negative. Confrontations generate negative emotions and may be felt for some time as residual feelings and moods.

We don't need to be living an event in order to experience the feelings associated with it. According to the research of Harvard psychologist Ellen Langer, remembered or imagined experiences can create the same flood of chemistry as the experience itself. This was substantiated in a 1993 American Medical Association Research Conference report which indicated that thinking about a stressful situation produces the same bodily and mental responses as experiencing it.

This explains why anticipating a confrontation can be just as distressing as experiencing one. It also explains why, even after we are no longer in the confrontive situation, we continue to experience the distress it produced.

The chemicals that produce our experience of distress must have time to dissipate. Here are some steps that we can take which permit us to manage our negative moods:

1. Buy yourself some time, and . . .

2. Fill this time with distractions (other work, relaxing or stimulating activities, etc.)

3. Understanding that it takes time for feelings to change, don't let them color or influence any other significant activity or undertaking.

Just Buy Yourself Some Time —

You may have noticed that each list of strategies suggested for "special confrontations" begins with: "Buy yourself some time." This relates to the difference between the rates at which the conscious and subconscious minds process information, the subconscious processing input much faster than the conscious. Nature has provided this difference so that, in survival or crisis situations, we can react quickly without having to think. We can get our foot on the brake pedal, our hands in front of our face, or our eyes closed without going through a conscious decision-making process.

These reactions keep us safe. However, all of our reactions are mechanically the same, including those to conflict. We can and often do react without thinking — without conscious control.

To take charge of these reactions, the first thing we have to learn is to buy ourselves some time. Time to allow the conscious mind to assess the situation, time to establish control first over ourselves and then over the environment. This can be accomplished by training ourselves to say something like, "I need some time to think about what has happened here," or "I would appreciate some time to consider what you have said." The time we "buy" may range from minutes to days, depending on the severity of the situation.

> Whether the confrontation is intra- or interpersonal in nature, buying time enough to take conscious control is the most significant thing you can do.

With the time we buy, we can monitor our feelings and hear what they are telling us. We can also listen to others and determine their positions and feelings. All of this helps us decide how to proceed to serve the best interests of everyone involved.

Whether the confrontation is intrapersonal or interpersonal, buying enough time to take conscious control is the most significant thing we can do.

HANDLING DIFFICULT PEOPLE

We will always encounter people with whom we are unable to get along. People who take exception to the things we say, or who resist us and our ideas. These may be the people whose support we need the most. Every time we have an encounter with people like this, we are in conflict.

It would be great if everyone we dealt with were skilled in managing conflicts and knew how best to confront them, but that's just not going to be the case. As a matter of fact, some people have developed ways of behaving that in and of themselves are confrontive. Sometimes diversity itself produces significant misunderstandings that can result in conflict. The whole idea of difficult people is a matter of perception. Remembering that our perceptions start the whole process of conflict, we must recognize that when we encounter a difficult individual it is because we perceive the person that way.

This is not to suggest that the perception isn't accurate, because it absolutely is — for us. The challenge is, what do we do with our perception? Sometimes as we get to know or understand a difficult person, perceptions change, but in the meantime, we need to be able to relate to this person as productively as possible.

The truth is, when dealing with a difficult person, every encounter may be a confrontation. So what do we do? First, remember all that we've said about effectively managing confrontations, especially the part about buying time. Next, remember that getting along with a difficult person is going to take reasonable accommodation. I say "reasonable" because some behaviors may be unacceptable and should not be tolerated. This is particularly true if the behaviors are demeaning or harassing in nature. If, on the other hand, the behaviors have to do with what we consider to be within the realm of propriety, then we need to take the initiative and manage the situation.

Finally, always remember that universal compatibility does not exist, and you needn't blame yourself when these kinds of situations occur. Instead, give yourself a pat on the back for taking charge of these situations and applying the tools you possess in an effort to manage them well.

7.

TAKING CHARGE OF
ORGANIZATIONAL CONFLICT

7. CONFLICT STRATEGIES

Our task in confrontations is to stabilize a conflict situation by diffusing emotions, containing the conflict to relevant issues, and taking a position of control. Having accomplished this, we can then move to the longer view where resolution of the conflict becomes the primary objective. However, before reviewing resolution strategies, we need to discuss the distinction between prevention and intervention, two very different dimensions of conflict.

Prevention is about reducing the number and frequency of conflicts, while intervention is usually aimed at reducing the severity of a conflict. Prevention affects intervention and vice versa.

Prevention

Understanding and awareness — prevention begins here. The most powerful deterrent to conflict is a solid understanding of the dynamics and nature of conflict as outlined in sections three and four. Organizational conflict begins with individuals. When individuals understand what conflict is, how it affects them, and the extent to which it directly or indirectly impacts the entire organization, they automatically treat it with greater respect.

> Prevention is about reducing the number and frequency of conflict . . . intervention is about reducing its severity.

Prevention hinges on the belief that having a clear understanding of conflict significantly reduces the number of conflicts and sets the stage for better management of those that develop. Prevention is far and away the most practical place to start taking charge of organizational conflict. The implications to the organization and its people of simply reducing the number of conflicts should be self-evident.

Painting Better Pictures — Many organizations now create primary management tools in the form of visions, missions, and/or strategic plans. The idea behind these tools is to focus the organization on achievable outcomes that not only serve the organization as a whole, but every member of the organization and every customer or customer group.

A common mistake in these undertakings is the failure to paint pictures in which members of the organization and customers see themselves portrayed as integral parts whose roles are critical to organizational outcomes. They must recognize personal benefits as well. Individuals need to see what's in it for them and how vital they are to making "it" happen.

Too often the vision, mission, or plan seems lofty and unrelated to each individual's day-to-day activities. People can't clearly and specifically identify either themselves or their roles in the big picture. This situation always produces conflict.

> Too often the vision, mission, or plan of the organization seems too lofty and unrelated to each individual's day-to-day activities.

A truly compelling mission, vision, or plan will, by its very nature, spell out individual roles and benefits, building what I refer to as "Compelling Images of Achievement." This is a way to productively marshal the people resources in an organization and tap into the generative potential of conflict at its highest level. When it comes to prevention, the greater clarity individuals in an organization have with respect to 1) what they are expected to do, 2) how what they do fits, and 3) why what they do is crucial to the success of the organization, the fewer conflicts arise.

Advocacy by Initiative — Few organizations today have sufficient resources to meet everyone's demands. Because of this, people and groups are competing for limited resources and this competition usually sparks some level of conflict. Actively promoting new ideas and change also produces conflict. Advocacy is an important tool for preventing conflict in organizational cultures facing any of these conditions. Advocacy by initiative is the process of proactively promoting needs or wants (desires). As we discussed in section three, through this type of advocacy it is possible to redirect the negative energy of factions into coalitions that are more closely aligned with the goals of the organization.

> Advocacy is about aligning your success with that of the person or entity that controls the resources you need to be successful.

The driving principles of advocacy by initiative are simple. The first step is to clearly define what is needed or wanted. The next step is to articulate that need or want in terms of the desired outcomes of those who can provide what is needed or wanted. As an example, if a department is seeking a larger budget, it must couch its request in language that demonstrates how having the specified additional resources will directly benefit the person or entity who controls the budget. In terms of the relationship between managers and staff, this principle can be stated as follows:

> Managers are driven by the desire to be perceived as successful by those outside the organization and above and below them in the organization.

The relationship matters less than the concept. If you are helping others to be successful and they understand that, they will be more sympathetic to your position. If they control the resources you need, this understanding can lead to redistribution of limited resources in your favor. This results from the second driving principle which is:

> In any organization, resources always flow to areas viewed as contributing to the success of the person(s) controlling the resources.

Advocacy by initiative is about aligning your success with that of the person or entity who controls the resources you need to be successful. The success of the controlling person or entity is then linked to your success and resources flow to you.

The interesting thing about advocacy is that at no time does it require that you take exception with the position of any other group or person. Rather than directly competing for resources, you are aligning your success with the success of the controlling person without having to be negative about individuals competing for the same resources.

One critical caveat exists with the use of advocacy by initiative. Since it appeals to the most significant individual motivator, self-interest, care must be given to what is being promised. When what has been promised by way of performance is delivered and has the anticipated result of enhancing success, a continued flow of resources can be expected. On the other hand, if results are not forthcoming or disappointing, considerable credibility is lost and with it any resource gains that may have been enjoyed.

Conflict Intervention

Intervention always begins with confrontation and then proceeds toward resolution. When a conflict does arise, the necessary first step is to engage in and take charge of the conflict through confrontation. Once this is accomplished using the tools and approaches developed in the last section, more deliberate approaches can then be applied to bring about resolution.

Remember that conflict resolution is the product of conflict management and the quality of the resolution is commensurate with the quality of the management. Remember, too, that only the conflicts in stages one and two are manageable. Conflicts that have escalated to stage three require interventions that are designed to establish or regain control of the situation before strategic management approaches have a chance of working. Finally, keep in mind that even at stages one and two, some conflicts turn out to be unresolvable. When a conflict is recognized to be unresolvable, the objective shifts to that of minimizing the damage and reaching accommodations that enable the parties involved to move past the conflict into more productive activities.

STRATEGIES FOR DEALING WITH CONFLICT

Most conflicts involve a dance — a series of moves and countermoves, with each party taking the lead or initiative at times and following or reacting at other times. Master conflict managers often learn to love the dance, to derive exhilaration and satisfaction from carefully defining the conflict, selecting and implementing strategies, observing their effects, and interpreting and responding to the behaviors of the other party.

> **The conscious mind must be engaged in the process of conflict resolution**

Conflict on this level can be like a well-matched game of chess, requiring intense energy and concentration, carefully calculated moves, and producing sometimes surprising and creative results. People who operate at this level have long since ceased to fear conflict; they sense challenge and opportunity, not threat, in the tension between opponents.

This book has been primarily devoted to developing an understanding of the nature of conflict, what causes it and what happens at cognitive and emotional levels while conflict is developing and playing out. A primary objective has been to gain conscious control of our own reactions by recognizing and seizing the cognitive moment that precedes conflict's emotional tidal wave, and to turn back the wave through the use of gateway skills. A second, related focus has been on the management of confrontations, recognizing that confrontation is the first step in the resolution process and a critical juncture that often determines who is in control and who is choreographing the dance — at least initially. This is a course in the basics.

Becoming adept at selecting and using conflict management strategies — at guiding and being guided gracefully across the floor — is more akin to graduate school. It would take another book to do justice to the subject by fully examining each strategy and discussing the interplay and possible effects of various moves in a variety of settings and circumstances. In this text, we merely list the more common strategies and provide a brief set of guidelines for each.

A strategy is a behavior or course of action that is consciously chosen for its ability to help reach a goal. When used unconsciously, the following approaches forfeit their status as strategies. Potentially effective behaviors can prove disastrous when applied randomly, carelessly, unconsciously, or inappropriately. The conscious mind must be engaged in the process of conflict resolution at all times.

The ultimate goal of any conflict management strategy is to transform the situation from a conflict that is emotionally charged to a problem that can be dealt with rationally and objectively. Here are ten strategies that can be consciously applied at any point in a conflict to bring about this transformation.

Depending on the nature of the conflict, different strategies will have varying degrees of utility. They are arranged in order from lowest (1.) to highest (10.) relative to the behavioral dimension of cooperation or collaboration.

Strategies at the low end of the scale tend to focus more directly on the issues, while those at the high end pay more attention to the relationships involved.

When choosing, and using, conflict strategies, always keep in mind that the other disputant(s) may also be employing strategies. A highly effective manager of conflict is skillful at 1) discerning whether behaviors on the part of the other party(ies) are consciously or unconsciously chosen, and 2) skillfully responding to conflict strategies coming from the other side of the table. Every strategy is a double edged sword. It can be used to your benefit, and it can sting, too.

1. Abandoning

Abandoning a conflict means, literally or figuratively, walking away from it. Some conflicts amount to pointless jousting with few or no consequences, good or bad. They are simply not worth your time and energy. Moreover, when you are terribly outnumbered, feel physically threatened, or find yourself in the middle of a conflict in which you do not wish to participate for personal, professional or ethical reasons, then abandonment can be effective.

Sample leads:

"Count me out folks. This isn't on my to-do list for today."

"Hey, this isn't worth a fight. Let's just forget it."

Cautions:

• In contrast to the strategies of avoiding and postponing, abandoning is a permanent solution. Be sure to observe this important differentiation. Don't say you are walking away from the conflict and then attempt to reassert your presence later with overt or covert attempts to influence the decision or situation.

• Don't abandon a conflict in the hopes that the other person(s) will come running after you, begging you to come back. If you make the decision to leave, be willing to accept the consequences of your action.

• Don't attempt to abandon serious conflicts. They will not abandon you.

2. Avoiding

One of the most common strategies for coping with conflict or potential conflict is avoidance. Avoidance is neither bad nor good, although it has garnered a somewhat negative reputation among those interested in conflict management.

Avoidance is typically practiced in the early stages of a relationship, when intimates or professional associates are first getting to know each other and prefer to concentrate on the positive features of their union.

When you stand to gain nothing from confronting a conflict, when power is drastically unequal, when you want to put distance between yourself and the other party, or when you just need time to prepare, avoidance is a legitimate strategy. Avoidance buys time. Use the time wisely once it is gained. For example, if you postpone a meeting, immediately get to work, prepare yourself, and reschedule. If you avoid a confrontation concerning an important issue, make an alternative plan for addressing the issue and follow through. When issues are not important, deferring action allows people to cool off, which is also an effective use of avoidance.

Sample leads:

"I have another obligation right now. Let's talk tomorrow."

"I need to look at all the facts. Can I get back to you on...?"

Cautions:

• On the negative side, by avoiding you may be perceived as "passing the buck" or sidestepping the issue. Be aware of this possibility — particularly if you tend to use this strategy frequently.

• If you notice the other party to the conflict avoiding, it might be a clue that he or she is uncertain and needs time to investigate the situation. However, if the other person is using avoidance beyond its potential for usefulness, you can:

— Communicate your hopes for resolving the conflict. Try to overcome the forces of fear and negativity by reassuring the other person that a win-win resolution is possible.

— If one person in a group is avoiding, let that individual off the hook. Separate the avoiding person from the problem if at all possible. Then move ahead with conflict resolution.

— Appeal to the avoider's sense of honesty. Seek out and define the reasons for resistance and inactivity.

— Limit the number of variables. Most conflicts have several parts. Factor the conflict issue into its most important sub-issues. Then deal with one at a time.

3. Dominating

Dominating is an effective strategy when a quick decision is needed or when the issue is relatively unimportant — it gets things done. Dominating is usually power-oriented and delivered with force.

The dominating style can actually be quite helpful when there is a general lack of knowledge or expertise on the part of the other parties to the conflict. Your ability to provide expert counsel or boldly address issues may be welcomed by the others. However, it is best to use this strategy sparingly. It's effectiveness lasts only as long a you have "right and might" on your side.

Sample leads:

"I understand your concerns. Now listen carefully to my assessment — I know what I'm talking about."

"There's too much going on right now. Just do what I've suggested, and everything will work out fine."

Caution:

The person who sets the rules gains power in a conflict. Pay attention if the other party attempts to control the agenda for a meeting or discussion, or insists that the issue be defined in a way that meets his or her needs more than yours. When you hear the message, "anything other than my preferred area of discussion is out of order," you are facing a person who intends to dominate the conflict by "prenegotiating" the issues.

4. Obliging

This strategy is used to deliberately elevate the other person, making him or her feel better about the situation. Obliging by raising another's status can be useful, especially if your role within the organization — and the conflict — is secure.

The obliging strategy plays down the differences between parties while seeking common ground. It can also be used if you are unsure of your position or fear a mistake has been made. By passively accepting the power of others, you buy time to assess the situation and survey alternatives.

By obliging, you give power to others. If your power is expendable, you can build trust and confidence in others by deferring occasionally. If you are secure in your position, use obliging as a means of delegation — yes, even in conflict.

Sample leads:

"I'm not an expert in this area. What do you think we should do?"

"I'm swamped with other demands right now, but I think this issue is very important. I'd trust you to come with some viable alternatives."

Cautions:

• When used effectively, obliging enhances relationships and creates good will. When used ineffectively, it signals insecurity, low self-esteem, passiveness, or (depending on what happens next), passive-aggression. Don't choose this strategy from a relatively weak position. You'll only get — and look — weaker.

• When the other party in a conflict is obliging toward you, take advantage of the additional power, while determining the person's motivation. Is he or she in a strong position and seeking to share power? Is he or she buying time to build a case while involving you in a pointless "busy-work?" Is this person frequently obliging toward others (a style) because of feelings of insecurity and low self-esteem that go beyond the issue at hand? Your answers to these questions should help prepare you for the next stage of the conflict.

5. Getting Help

More accurately called "seeking intervention," this strategy involves getting a third party to act as a conflict mediator. Not every conflict can or should be resolved by the disputants acting alone. If collaboration is unlikely or the situation is unresolvable because of disparate skills, highly charged emotions, language barriers, or blatant uncooperativeness by one or more parties, help is required. Arbitration or mediation is always needed if one party threatens in any way to retaliate against the other.

Depending on the seriousness of the conflict and the potential consequences of the resolution, the person performing the intervention service can be anyone from a skillful listener/communicator to a professional mediator, just as long as he or she is unbiased, neutral, and respectful of both (or all) parties involved in the conflict.

Awareness and control are required to even suggest this strategy. Consequently, the more skillful, assertive, confident disputant will likely be the first to recognize intervention as an alternative. If that is you, suggesting a neutral third party must be motivated by nothing less than your commitment to finding a win-win resolution.

Sample leads:

"I think we should ask someone to sit in with us and help us resolve this issue."

"I have asked Ms. Romero to join us today, because I think she can help us sort this thing out. Is that all right with you?"

Caution:

When the other party in a conflict proposes to bring in a third party, consider that he or she may be attempting to form or expand a faction. Even a rigorously neutral interventionist will have the effect of increasing the power of the weakest party through facilitating communication and equalizing input between parties. When anyone less than neutral enters into the relationship of two people in order to help manage a conflict, it is extremely difficult for that person to not form a closer bond with one of the parties compared to the other. One of the most natural tendencies of any triad is to subdivide into a dyad plus one.

6. Humor

Using humor to diffuse a conflict situation can be particularly effective when the disputants are peers, and when the conflict is not terribly serious. Being humorous may involve looking at the situation in a comical way, jokingly acknowledging a style of reacting that frequently gets you into trouble, or generally making light of the situation.

Sample leads:

"Do you think I should dial 911 before we start, just to save time?"

"There I go again. In a former life I was a Spanish Inquisitor, you know."

Cautions:

• The use of humor is inadvisable when the other person(s) is very upset, or when you clearly have the power in the situation.

• When a person responds consistently with jokes, teasing, sarcasm, or humorous self-deprecation, he or she is displaying a style — probably one of avoidance. The jokester's unconscious purpose may be to distract people from serious issues, to avoid the work of negotiation and collaboration, or to gain power by monopolizing time and energy.

7. Postponing

Postponing is putting off till tomorrow what neither you nor the other party to the conflict are prepared to deal with today. It differs from avoiding in that it is a low-level, handshake type of preliminary agreement. This is good. The ability to jointly agree to put off dealing with a conflict until both parties have cooled off, are more rested, and/or have their facts straight requires control and a definite degree of skill.

Postponement works best when several conditions are present. First of all, be sure to acknowledge the emotional content of the conflict even while deferring other issues to a later time. "I can see you're upset, however . . ."

When you postpone dealing with a conflict, do so openly and in collaboration with the other person(s) involved. This is a strategy, not an escape hatch. Before going your separate ways, establish the time and place of your next contact or meeting.

Sample leads:

"I'm simply not up to this right now. Can we meet tomorrow?"

"I think we're both too upset to be effective. Let's talk on Friday, after we've had a few days to calm down."

Cautions:

• Postponement does not work well if the other people involved think they are being put off, never to return to the issue. Statements such as a vague, "we'll have to work on this later," or "let's all try harder to get along," are often give-aways that the person making the statement has no intention of voluntarily coming back to the conflict issue. When you are in a conflict and hear statements like these coming from the other party, it's your cue to strongly reaffirm your commitment to resolving the conflict and insist on setting a date and time for doing so.

• Don't postpone a conflict when all parties demonstrate the energy and desire to work out the conflict immediately. If you postpone (or let the other party postpone) without good reason, you run the risk of wasting a valuable resource — emotional investment. When the time and energy are available for working out an issue, go ahead and deal with it.

8. Compromise

This strategy assumes a middle-of-the-road orientation. In compromise, everyone has something to give and something to take.

Compromise is most effective when issues are complex and/or when there is a balance of power. Compromise can be chosen when other methods have failed and when both parties are looking for middle ground, willing to exchange concessions. It almost always means all parties giving up something in order to attain part of what they want, as well as resolution to the conflict.

Negotiation and bargaining are complementary skills in compromising. The advantage of compromise is that it gets people talking about the issues and moves them closer to each other and to a resolution.

Sample leads:

"Obviously, we have different opinions. What is the bottom line for you?"

"We're each going to have to give a little in order settle this issue. Let's see what we can come up with."

Cautions:

• Compromise works best when both or all parties to the conflict are "right," but simply have different values or opinions. It doesn't work well at all when one side is clearly wrong. You wouldn't advise an employee or colleague to compromise with a sexual harraser.

• Before entering into a compromise, be clear in your own mind concerning which of your needs/wants relative to the conflict are negotiable and which are not.

9. Integrating

Integrating is similar to collaboration, with an emphasis on the exchange and/or pooling of information. The objective is to examine differences and to weigh all factors and data that may ultimately impinge on a resolution. This strategy is typically associated with problem-solving and is highly desirable when issues are complex.

Integrating encourages creative thinking and welcomes input from diverse perspectives. It rallies parties to find solutions to complex issues. Developing alternatives is one strength of this strategy. Integrating is an efficient and effective segue to collaboration and problem solving.

Sample leads:

"Let's meet with everyone involved and really look at what's going on."

"This is obviously a complex issue. Let's see if we can sort it out."

Cautions:

• Integration is not an effective strategy when a party lacks commitment or when the deadline is tight. Integration takes time.

• Since integrating ignites cognitive mechanisms, a skilled conflict manager may use it to subdue emotional reactions. However, if the emotional content of the conflict is extremely high, integrating may be difficult, because reason and rational considerations are likely to be overshadowed by anger, frustration, fear, etc. In other words, integrating probably won't work very well if people really want to fight.

• Having someone ask you to go "gather all the facts" may strike you as a cold, uncaring response when what you want to do first is unload strong feelings. Feelings — yours and those of the other parties in a conflict — should never be completely ignored.

• When gathering and sharing information, be careful not to leave anyone out. An excluded person may become very offended, causing problems later.

10. Collaboration

Collaborating means working together to resolve the conflict, and involves application of some variation of the problem-solving process, as well as the strategy of Integration. In order to collaborate, each party to the conflict must be ready and willing to take responsibility for finding a resolution, and must contribute equitably to the time, energy, resources, planning, and action required. Cooperation is a two-way street. You can't expect others to be cooperative if you always have to have your way.

In collaboration, all parts of the conflict must be accurately defined to the satisfaction of both (or all) disputants. Information must be gathered (Integration), enlarging the pool of potential alternatives. When as much is known about the issue as can be reasonably expected, alternative resolutions are generated, and a win-win resolution is chosen.

Sample leads:

"Both of us deserve to feel good about what happens. That means we're going to have to work side by side to find the best solution."

"Together, we can't fail to work this out. We've got the resources and we're both committed to finding a solution."

Cautions:

• When dealing with complex issues, keep in mind that there are probably several parts to the underlying problem. All of those parts must be successfully addressed by the chosen alternative, or the conflict will not be completely resolved.

The collaborative solution is usually the most productive in organizations. Collaboration requires trust, but at the same time it produces trust as parties to the conflict focus on achieving a cooperative solution. Because so much of the success of collaboration rides on the ability to solve problems, the development of problem-solving skills should be a prerequisite.

PROBLEM SOLVING

Problem solving, like conflict, is a process. It is an integral part of resolution and is the aim of all the tools, approaches, and strategies we bring to bear in dealing with confrontations and conflict. Here is a useful illustration of the process and an excellent reference to review when problems need to be solved:

Problem-Solving Flow Chart

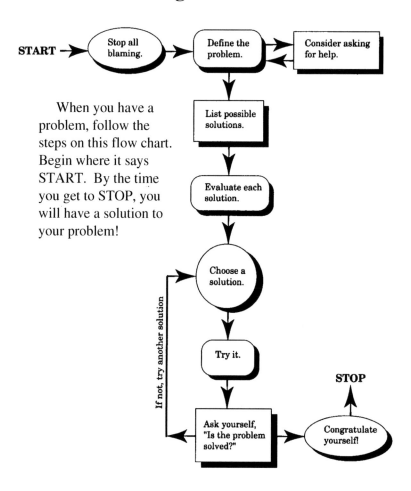

When you have a problem, follow the steps on this flow chart. Begin where it says START. By the time you get to STOP, you will have a solution to your problem!

The Steps for Responsibly Solving a Problem.

1. Focus on the problem. Stop any attempts to fix blame on circumstances or people (Rule of Objectivity).

2. Define the problem. Part of this step involves examining the nature, source, and dynamics of the problem (conflict).

3. Determine what resources are necessary to solve the problem and whether or not they are readily available. Decide if the assistance of others must be solicited. (Take time to re-examine the strategy of "Integration.")

4. Focus on outcomes while considering possible solutions.

5. Consider the consequences of each alternative solution. Get more information if necessary. Keeping in mind the concept of win/win, evaluate each alternative in terms of its individual and collective impact.

6. Decide on one or a combination of alternatives to implement. This is where an understanding of consensus-building is useful. Remember that in building consensus we do not need unanimous agreement that the alternative selected is absolutely the best one. Consensus requires only that everyone agree to support the selection and give it a chance to work. Agreement also needs to be reached regarding evaluation of the solution after it has been given a fair trial.

7. Implement the solution. This takes planning. Decide what steps need to be taken, as well as how and when to take them.

8. Evaluate the effectiveness of the solution based on the degree to which it solves the problem. Allow optimal time for the solution to work; then promptly evaluate. If the problem has not been resolved or has been only partially resolved, go back to the alternatives and select a new one (resuming the process at Step 6).

When you have successfully resolved the conflict, congratulate yourself. Why? Because you have consciously, thoughtfully, and deliberately accomplished a feat that some people never experience in a lifetime. Successfully moving through conflict is a significant achievement, warranting affirmation, reinforcement, and celebration.

TRY THIS!

When a conflict is transformed into its most manageable state, it becomes a problem to solve. Use this activity to give people hands-on experience with the problem-solving process and to provide opportunities to generate and evaluate solutions to hypothetical and real problems.

You will need clippings of a newspaper advice column (e.g., "Dear Abby" or "Ann Landers") and 4" by 6" index cards. In addition you should reproduce the Problem-Solving Flow Chart on page 139 on a chalk board or chart paper so that everyone can see it.

From the advice column, read a typical problem to the participants without reading the columnist's response. Instead, ask participants to think of the response they would give. Provide 2 minutes. Then ask a few of the participants how they would solve the problem. Ensure that the responses make sense, and then ask two or three people how they arrived at their solutions. Note the steps (if any) on the chalkboard or chart paper.

Have the participants organize into small groups of no more than six. Take a few minutes and, using "The Steps for Responsibly Solving a Problem" discussed earlier, review the flow chart so that everyone understands it. Give each group a copy of a second problem from the advice column (the same problem for each group).

Give the groups 10 minutes to apply the problem-solving steps. Have them record their solution on a 4" by 6" card. When the groups have all completed their work, read the problem aloud, and ask representatives from the various groups to share the solution they selected.

To complete the activity, generate a discussion with the following questions:

— *What did you learn from solving another person's problem?*

— *Why is it important to define the problem correctly?*

— *How difficult was it to generate alternative solutions?*

— *If the first solution doesn't work, what should you do?*

— *How is this process like the one you use to solve your own problems? How is it different?*

Developing skills as a conflict manager and problem solver has implications that reach far beyond the organization. These skills extend to our personal lives; they have efficacy in every area of existence. The secret to their development is not simply having an awareness of them or knowing how important they are. The secret is in rehearsing and practicing them on a regular basis and then debriefing every conflict in terms of how well we were able to manage it. The point of this exercise is not to highlight failures, but to identify learnings so that each new conflict becomes a learning opportunity or "teachable moment." The same holds true for development of the same skills in an organizational context. In our relief at having a conflict behind us, let's not fail to take advantage of its lessons.

COMMUNICATING STRATEGICALLY

The existence of good communications in an organization greatly enhances the skills of conflict management. Of particular importance is the willingness and ability of individuals to listen "actively" to one another — not just for the content conveyed, but for feelings as well. Good listeners have a real advantage as conflict managers.

Good speakers have an advantage, too. Four essential speaking skills you can use during conflict are called **The Four C's**:

• **Speak Clearly.** One if the best ways to ensure clarity is to slow your pace. (Caution: When you slow down, keep your tone *up!*)

• **Speak Concisely.** Get your point across in a reasonable amount of time. Remember the famous words of Earl Nightingale: "Talk is cheap. Supply always exceeds demand."

• **Choose Words Correctly.** Conflict management will be easier if you can express exactly what you mean and feel. In particular, developing a vocabulary of "feeling words" is tantamount to making regular deposits in your conflict readiness account.

• **Use Concrete Terminology.** Nothing is ever accomplished when your message is unclear; speak to be understood. Avoid overusing pronouns (it, them, we, us, that, etc.). Frequently, listeners have no idea (or have to guess) what you are referring to; use names, labels, titles, and specific terms instead.

All organizations and every individual can benefit from enhancing communications skills with the Four C's; however, one skill remains that has enormous value in conflict situations at any stage. The "I" message, described more than twenty years ago by psychologist Dr. Thomas Gordon, is an assertive skill that is essential to problem solving and to all the collaborative conflict-resolution strategies.

DEVELOPING THE USE OF "I" MESSAGES

In the course of dealing with interpersonal conflict, we must confront situations and behaviors that we find unacceptable. Delivering an "I" message rather than a "you" message can make the difference between effective and ineffective communication, and between a confrontation that de-escalates rather than escalates a conflict.

"I sure get upset and discouraged when we fail to meet our deadlines," is more effective than, "You're always missing deadlines. Aren't you ever going to learn to take responsibility?" A "you" message is usually interpreted by others to mean that they are in some way deficient or incompetent. "You" messages put people on the defensive and almost always provoke resistance to changing the behavior in question. Instead of communicating that there is something wrong with the other person, an "I" message simply lets the other person know YOUR feelings. Honestly conveying to others the effect their behavior has on you can be highly effective at bringing about change. Imagine the reactions of a recipient to the messages in these two lists.

"You" Messages	**"I" Messages**
You need to be more accurate. You make too many mistakes.	I feel nervous when I'm not certain about accuracy.
You're acting like a prima donna. Stop trying to steal the show.	I get frustrated when teamwork breaks down.
You've got to change your behavior, or I'll . . .	It's really hard for me when I have to deal with behavior like this.
Why don't you ever . . .	When things like this happen, it makes me crazy.
You're always complaining. Why can't you ever be satisfied?	I'm really upset by the all the disruption this complaining is causing.

"You" Messages Disguised As "I" Messages

When giving an "I" message, describe the other person's behavior and share your feelings honestly, explaining how the behavior affects you. A word of caution: Beware of the "you" message disguised as an "I" message. Always remember to focus on your feelings and on the results of the behavior. Most "you" messages begin with the focus on the individual and the message almost always contains the word "you" or "your." Notice the examples of "you" messages just presented.

When a "you" message is disguised as an "I" message, it might begin with the focus on your feelings, but look at what happens during the rest of the message: "I'm really upset by all the disruption (great "I" message so far) YOUR (oops!) complaining is causing." Look back at the last "I" message in our examples. See how easily we slipped that "your" into our message? What began as an effective "I" message became an ineffective and destructive "you" message by just substituting "your" for "this" in the statement.

In an "I" message, the focus is on your feelings in response to the behavior of others. A "you" message focuses on the other person and usually says little about your feelings. Letting others know the effects their behavior has on you is less threatening than is the implication that they are somehow bad or deficient because of their behavior.

TRY THIS!

Provide each person with a sheet listing the following situations and "you " messages. Ask them to read each situation and the related "you" message, then write an appropriate "I" message.

Situation: You are trying to explain something to one of your colleagues and he or she keeps interrupting.

"You" message: You never listen!

Situation: Your secretary cleaned out a file drawer and, without checking, threw out some important papers.

"You" message: You're so careless. Why don't you ever ask before you do things?

Situation: One of your fellow workers is playing a radio so loudly that it is disturbing you.

"You" message: Why do you have to play that so loud? You're never considerate of others.

Situation: Your friend didn't show up on time to meet you after work and you had to wait.

"You" message: I can never trust you. You told me to meet you at 5 o'clock and then you didn't have the courtesy to be on time.

Situation: Your boss sets up a meeting, but you're not prepared.

"You" message: Why do you always do this to me. You never check to see if I'm ready.

Provide adequate time for everyone to complete the task and then ask a number of individuals to share their "I" messages with the group.

Now ask the participants to take a moment and think of a recent situation, either personal or professional, in which they could have used an "I" message. Have them write this message. Don't ask them to share these messages; however do facilitate a discussion with the following question:

— *How difficult do you think it would be to create an "I" message habit as a way of responding in difficult situations? In what ways would it be worth the effort?*

It's okay to have feelings. In fact they are essential. It's also okay — even healthy — to express those feelings. Feelings start out as messengers telling us about the quality of our relationship with the environment. Through good communication, we then use our feelings to let others know what we are experiencing. In this way our feelings continue to deliver their message. What we should not do is turn our feelings into weapons with which to bludgeon others. Developing the skill of formulating and delivering "I" messages will assist us in every relationship we ever have. By assisting others to develop this skill, we offer the same promise to them.

Certainly, we must confront conflict situations, but it is vital to offset these confrontations with expressions that focus on the conflict situation while at the same time actively recognizing positive behavior using descriptive and appreciative praise. Furthermore, the potential damage of negative confrontations can be significantly reduced or converted to positive growth by using "I" messages instead of "you" messages. In this manner it is possible to remove the "negative" from negative confrontations and produce positive experiences for everyone involved.

If we consistently catch people doing things right and take advantage of confrontations as teachable moments, we'll be doing much to develop important skills and to enhance healthy, positive, and growing relationships.

SUMMARY

The management of conflict proceeds in a natural flow directed

---

Think about this . . .

As an aside, there is a striking similarity between giving descriptive, appreciative praise and "I" messages. In both cases, you are describing the results of someone else's behavior and the effect it has on you. *You keep the focus on the action and not the actor.* As you can see, "I" messages are woven into effective praise for positive behavior just as they are into effective confrontation of negative behavior.

by the awareness, knowledge, and skill of the conflict manager.

Important first steps in organizations of any kind, families included, are giving people a general understanding of the dynamics (effects) and nature (mechanics) of conflict and supplementing these understandings with a specific awareness of what happens to each of us when we are in conflict. With just this information, individuals are better able to take charge of themselves in conflict situations. Even if nothing more is taught, the frequency and severity of conflict will go down.

If, in addition, time is taken to develop the skills associated with managing confrontations, even greater reductions will be realized. Finally, if organizations undertake in-depth training to develop the strategies for effectively managing conflict once it has been stabilized and contained, not only will the number and severity of conflicts be further reduced, organizations will position themselves to take advantage of the generative potential offered by each new conflict situation.

Is it worth the investment? Conflict presents us with enormous opportunities to conserve and to create resources. Taken together, these should be justification enough.

8.

TAKING CHARGE OF
ORGANIZATIONAL CONFLICT

8. THE ART & SCIENCE OF MEDIATION

You may be the most patient, peace-loving person in the world — rarely a conflict with anyone, committed to fostering cooperation and fairness — and still find yourself dealing with conflict on a somewhat regular basis. In spite of your values and easygoing nature, occasionally it will be necessary to intervene in conflicts between disgruntled employees or combatant colleagues, taking the role of a neutral third party — a mediator.

IN THE MIDDLE

A *mediator* is someone who helps to reconcile, settle, or resolve differences between disputants. A *mediation* is a mediator's attempt to bring about a peaceful settlement or compromise through objective intervention. Situations which might occasion donning the mediator robe vary from isolated battles over specific issues to long-running guerrilla wars based on personality clashes, values differences, petty jealousies, job-based resentments, simple misunderstandings and viscous vendettas. The mechanisms by which you can become involved, however, are fairly predictable.

> Sudden and sometimes heated flare-ups are bound to occur in any environment where individuals regularly team up or interface to get the job done.

OPEN SKIRMISHES.

Sudden and sometimes heated flare-ups are bound to occur in any environment where individuals regularly team up or interface to get the job done. Most of the time they burn themselves out quickly and without the need for intervention. However, occasionally you may decide to step in — or you may be drawn in. For example:

Shouts, curses, and loud accusations are coming from the office or cubicle of a worker. The noise is plainly disrupting the work of others, which you interpret it as your cue. Knocking on the wall or door as you enter the area, you interrupt with something like, "Excuse me, what's going on here," and proceed...

Or... you're about to head out for a meeting when a visibly agitated employee intercepts you and blurts out, "I've had it up to here with Curtis. I don't care what happens, I want off his team!" Unhesitatingly, you respond "Okay, where's Curtis? Let's get him in here and we'll talk about it right now."

So there you are with two opponents in the same room. What next? The first step is to quickly assess the emotional intensity of the conflict. If the situation is too explosive for productive discussion (stage three or close to it), stop the battle but postpone any attempt at mediation. Buy some time by suggesting, "Obviously you're both pretty upset right now. Why don't we meet back here at two after you've had a chance to calm down."

On the other and, if the disputants have their emotions reasonably under control, commence your prelude to mediation. (We'll get into the exact process and suggested "leads" to discussion later on.)

The risk of postponing mediation is that one or both parties will *not* spend the time calming down, but instead go forth and spew anger wherever and at whomever they encounter. Contrary to popular belief, when it comes to anger "letting it all out" is *not* helpful. Acting on anger will generally make a person angrier, and each angry outburst will prolong and deepen the distress. So, if you can, get the parties to agree to the confidentiality rule right away ("Establish a contract," page 180) and then urge them to get their minds off the situation during the interim by either getting back to work or engaging in some stress-reducing activity like eating lunch or taking a walk.

GUERRILLA WARFARE

Lots of conflicts live underground. You can't see them

exactly, but you can sense them. Sometimes two people can work alongside each other for months or even years in a state of unacknowledged conflict. On the surface they appear calm and rational, but underneath they are churning with resentment, jealousy, guilt, fear, or frustration. This kind of situation is stressful not just for the people directly involved, but for everyone around them.

Arguably, as long as goals are being accomplished and people are getting their work done, such disquiet is none of your business. You may abhor having your workers locked in a cold war, but they have a right to their disputes. However, if productivity is affected, you won't want to wait too long before getting involved.

The first thing you need to do in circumstances like these — and in all potential mediation situations — is demonstrate your respect for and confidence in the ability of people to solve their own problems. Don't issue orders and edicts, and don't immediately intervene and impose the wisdom of your vast experience by providing a solution to the problem. For one thing, unless you are very astute and have been observing the conflict for a long time, you won't know what the real issues are until the disputants have confronted them in your presence.

> You need to demonstrate your respect for and confidence in the ability of people to solve their own problems

When you are ready to intervene in a guerrilla conflict, the best approach is to let each disputant know, separately, that you are aware a problem exists, and are concerned about specific effects (cite them) that the conflict is having on productivity, morale, etc. Then offer to help.

If the person is open to discussing the situation with you in this private one-to-one setting, start by just listening. When you think you've listened enough, listen a little longer. (It's almost impossible for most of us to over listen.) When you are reasonably confident that you have demonstrated to the person's satisfaction your grasp of the problem *from his or her perspective*, ask the person to think of some things he or she might do to help resolve the conflict. These are actions that *this one individual* can take, *not* attempts to change the other person. For example you might ask, "What if anything might you do, Javier, to make things better? Forget Rick for now — what can *you* do on your own?"

If Javier comes up with some good ideas, consider allowing him to implement one or two of them for a few days or weeks before proceeding further. If not, it's time to look at other alternatives. One of the alternatives is mediation. Suggest it. If the problem is severe or its effects far reaching, *strongly* suggest it.

CLASHES BETWEEN OR AMONG YOUR PEERS

Open skirmishes and hidden hostilities sometimes occur within the management team, jeopardizing the effectiveness of planning, decision making, and other leadership functions. The same basic guidelines apply, accept that you seldom have to convince anyone that you won't use your authority to impose a solution, because authority over your peers is limited or lacking in the first place. You may have the power to influence them, but that power comes from sources other than a higher position within the organization.

So you initiate a confrontation by saying something like, "Jake and Linda, you two have been at each other's throats for weeks. I think it's important to the effectiveness of our management team that you set aside some time to pinpoint the cause of your conflict and then do whatever it takes to resolve it. And if you think you'd benefit from a mediator, I'm available."

UNABASHED INVITATIONS

Once in a great while, people in conflict actually take the initiative in setting up a mediation. They let you know, directly or indirectly, concisely or "in so many words," that they could use some help. The less direct the message, the more your listening skills will determine the outcome; however, assuming the message is decoded correctly, all you have to say is , "Of course, I'd be glad to help," or "Sounds like you could use an unbiased third person to help you with this. Would I do?"

FEAR OF CONFRONTATION

A common reason for not dealing directly with conflict is the fear of confrontation, a fear that rarely exists solely in the minds of the disputants. Often, people around the disputants also fear a confrontation and subtly or blatantly discourage it. Potential mediators beware: To serve as a mediator, you must be capable of accepting and even *encouraging* confrontation.

> To serve as a mediator, you must be capable of accepting and even *encouraging* confrontation.

Confrontation brings conflict into the open and defines it. Disputants can't hide or deny a conflict and confront it at the same time. Confronting a conflict usually involves one person confronting the other — stating complaints, points of disagreement, and feelings. This can be difficult to do, and even more difficult to do well.

Confrontation may occur prior to a mediation or as an initial step in mediation, but it must occur.

HOW TO MEDIATE A CONFLICT

When you assume the role of mediator, your job is to be an objective facilitator of the process of painstaking clarification, focused creativity, and consensus. You must:
- listen to both (or all) sides
- ask questions to facilitate mutual understanding
- stay neutral and refrain from judging or taking sides

• ensure confidentiality

• help people find a solution to their problem

The mediation process consists of the seven steps listed here. Each step is examined more fully below:

STEPS IN MEDIATION

1. Establish a contract.
2. Define the problem.
3. Ask for concessions.
4. Brainstorm solutions.
5. Evaluate solutions.
6. Choose a solution.
7. Get agreement.

1. Establish a contract.

The purpose of a contract is to clarify the ground rules for mediation. Remind the disputants that, just as opponents in a chess game or tennis match must observe rules, so must disputants in a conflict. Point by point, insist that the disputants agree to:

• listen

• respect each other

• avoid arguing and putting each other down

• work together to find a solution to the conflict

• keep what transpires confidential

Besides setting the stage for a productive mediation, establishing a contract takes a tremendous burden off of you as a facilitator. Now, instead of having to play psychologist or master mediator, trained in the subtleties of human interaction, your main job is to ensure that the disputants follow the rules — that they listen to each other, are respectful of one another's feelings and perspectives, and that they stay on task by focusing on solutions rather than who is right or wrong, victim or villain.

2. Define the problem.

If a confrontation has not occurred prior to the mediation, this is it. Give each person an uninterrupted opportunity to describe the problem from his or her point of view. When both have spoken, restate and clarify until you arrive at a mutually acceptable definition of the problem.

One of the most effective ways for disputants to confront a difficult or complicated conflict is by combining two very effective communication techniques: I-statements and active listening. The problem (or a portion thereof) is described by each disputant in the form of an I-statement ("I feel...," "I am upset about...," "When such-and-such happens, I can't do my job...," etc.). The same disputant is then guided to listen carefully while the other person responds and then to immediately restate the essence of the response. This combination is repeated over and over again by both disputants until the entire problem has been defined.

3. Ask for concessions.

Ask the disputants what each of them is willing to do to resolve the parts of the problem for which they are responsible. They should make suggestions about their own behavior, not the other person's.

This valuable step is preliminary to actual problem solving; its beauty is that it gives each disputant an opportunity to take responsibility for behaviors that have contributed to the problem and volunteer to change those behaviors.

4. Brainstorm solutions.

Help the disputants think of alternatives. Write them down. Don't allow any criticism or evaluation of alternatives during brainstorming. Encourage creativity and innovation throughout this phase of the process.

5. Evaluate solutions.

Discuss each alternative, assessing its costs and benefits. Consider how it will affect *all* of the people involved. Above all, judge its ability to solve the problem.

If the problem is a compound problem — one with several parts — clearly identify which parts of the issue are addressed by each alternative.

6. Choose a solution.

Help the disputants agree on a solution (one or a combination of alternatives) that both are willing to try. Stress that the solution should be the best of available alternatives, but does not have to be perfect. Solutions that prove unsatisfactory or solve only part of the problem can be amended later.

7. Get agreement.

Ask for a commitment from both parties to make a sincere effort to implement the solution and see it through. Write down the solution, ask both disputants to sign it, and give each a copy.

HELPFUL PHRASES TO USE IN MEDIATION

All of us worry about knowing the right thing to say, particularly in a conflict situation. Here are some very useful phrases that you can use or adapt:

- *How do you think the two of you should handle this?*
- *Mary has a problem she'd like to discuss with you, Li.*
- *What do you think a fair solution would be?*
- *The two of you need to talk about this, and I'd like to help. When is a good time for you?*
- *Let's talk this over so the two of you can...*
- *Perhaps you can find a solution that will satisfy both of you.*
- *Obviously you don't agree with each other. Would you like to talk about it?*
- *I think we should wait till you both get all the facts before we try to settle this.*
- *We'll be able to discuss this much better when the shouting is over and everyone has calmed down.*
- *Why are you so opposed to _____'s idea?*

TRAINING OTHERS AS MEDIATORS

Depending on your position in the organization, you may be satisfied to add mediation skills to your own repertoire, periodically performing a mediation and sharpening these tools in the process.

On the other hand, you may be (or become) such a fan of mediation that you want to promote its benefits throughout the organization, *without* getting stuck in the role of universal practitioner. A possible solution is to train a group of employees to act as *peer mediators*.

If you work in a mid- to large-size organization, your human resources department probably conducts regular training programs in a variety of areas, and the logical approach would be to work with the HR manager to add mediation training to current offerings. If your organization is small, you will either have to designate an individual to develop and coordinate a peer mediation program or do it yourself.

IDENTIFYING VOLUNTEER MEDIATORS

There are two basic approaches to forming a group of peer mediators. One is to select first and train only designated mediator candidates; the other is to train anyone who signs up and select based on demonstrated competency at the conclusion of training. Either approach works. The advantage of the select-train method is that it places mediators in specific locations throughout the organization while conserving training resources. The advantages of the train-select method are that it 1) dispenses valuable conflict-resolution and problem-solving skills throughout the organization, and 2) sends the message that the skills of mediation are an organizational priority.

To identify mediators using the select-train method, ask for supervisor recommendations or simply advertise the opportunity to everyone and then screen and interview the applicant pool. Look for individuals who are:

• well-liked and respected by their peers
• good listeners and communicators
• in positions with reasonable time flexibility so that they can be available to mediate.

In addition, consider such questions as whether to designate one mediator for each department, how often to rotate mediators, and whether you want mediators to work singly or in teams of two. Since most conflicts involve two disputants, having two mediators creates not only symmetry but support, easing the pressure on both individuals.

MEDIATOR TRAINING

Mediators should receive training in:

• the nature and dynamics of conflict (covered in this book)
• the policy of the organization to promote peaceful win-win resolution to conflicts
• the mediation process
• listening skills
• the problem-solving process

Provide mediator-trainees abundant opportunities to rehearse the mediation process. Case-study videos are useful for viewing the process in action, practicing problem identification, and critiquing the decisions and skills of the mediators portrayed. When it comes to actual practice, nothing beats role-playing. Develop a dozen or more conflict scenarios, assign roles, and have mediator-trainees act out the parts of disputants and mediators. Allow plenty of time for debriefing, reassign roles, and repeat using the same scenario or a new one.

Active mediators should meet at least twice a month for discussion, debriefing by human resources staff (or the program coordinator), and ongoing training. Focus continued training on the honing of communication and problem-solving skills. Later on, mediators might benefit by examining community volunteer mediation programs, such as court programs, and/or commercially available mediation courses.

SHARPEN THE SAW

To avoid burnout, rotate mediators every six to twelve months — more frequently if they are under exceptional stress. Recognize and encourage mediators through standard incentive programs, employee-of-the-month awards and other types of honors.

INFORMING STAFF OF THE MEDIATION ALTERNATIVE

The possibility of mediation will eventually become known via the office grapevine to everyone in the organization, but you can speed this awareness with a printed or electronic bulletin. In addition to summarizing company policy concerning mediation and the goals of your particular mediation program, outline the service in simple straightforward terms, as in the following example:

What Is mediation?

Mediation is when people who are in conflict agree they want to solve the problem, and meet with trained mediators who help them find a solution. Mediators listen to both sides and remain neutral while helping people in conflict find a solution to their problem. Mediators always keep what is said in mediation private.

Who are mediators?

• Fellow employees who have volunteered and been trained to listen and facilitate without taking sides.
• Your coworkers and friends in the company who want to help.

Why mediate?

• To settle problems before they affect your job.
• To work out a solution to your problem instead of having your supervisor decide what will happen.
• Because mediators, who are your peers, understand many of the pressures of the job and can empathize with your feelings, needs, and goals.

HOW TO ARRANGE FOR A MEDIATION:

• Tell your supervisor or boss that you desire mediation.
• Tell a mediator.
• Tell someone in human resources.
• Fill out a mediation-request form located in...

THE BENEFITS OF CONFLICT MEDIATION

As your individual and/or programmatic mediation efforts mature, gain acceptance, and grow in use throughout the organization, you will notice a number of positive side effects. Appropriate evaluation instruments and feedback mechanisms are likely to record:

• fewer disciplinary actions
• better communication
• improved morale
• greater productivity

With each successful outcome, the reputation of mediation as a viable alternative will grow. Employees involved in conflicts that they are unable to settle independently will seek out mediation because they know it works.

9.

TAKING CHARGE OF
ORGANIZATIONAL CONFLICT

9. IMPORTANT PROCESSES

Two very useful processes are presented in this section as additional resources for enhancing organizational communication and development. Although they have wide general application, they are particularly useful in the realm of conflict. The first is the Group Work Circle. The second is the Comprehensive Feedback Model.

GROUP WORK CIRCLES

The Group Work Circle is a unique small-group discussion process in which members follow an established procedure and adhere to a few basic rules as they talk about a specific topic. Topics may relate to issues or tasks currently being dealt with by the organization as a whole, or their purpose may be to facilitate the growth of the group, by encouraging sharing, awareness, self-disclosure, mutual acceptance, dialogue and positive interaction. The Group Work Circle is an elegant, proven process and is equally effective when used as a problem-solving tool, a team-building strategy, or a venue for ongoing dialogue.

The value of dialogue is tacitly if not explicitly recognized in most organizations. Witness the frequency of meetings and the constant flow of information, the questions, reactions, and alternative views — the rumors, prophecies, and lunchroom debates. In effective organizations, dialogue is always encouraged; however, when discussion is random, certain people tend to get left out. Some are shy or insecure, others introspective, still others just too busy. Even scheduled discussions open to everyone frequently end up excluding the least verbal, least assertive members of a group. What makes the Group Work Circle unique is that its structure, procedure, and rules assure every individual equal time, equal consideration, and equal respect. And since the most creative ideas and solutions are just as likely to come from the unassertive as the outspoken, the entire organization benefits.

Goals of the Group Work Circle

> Either we're pulling together or we're pulling apart.

All Group Work Circles share a set of general goals that relate to the development and expression of intrapersonal and interpersonal excellence. These are goals of every circle, no matter what the topic. In a sense, they are prerequisite goals. Through their attainment the group is empowered to achieve the more specific goals implied by the circle's topic or objective.

General Goals

- To open avenues of communication
- To build trust
- To develop awareness of self and others
- To develop positive interaction skills
- To encourage quality listening, and the use of other communication skills

More specific goals are established when the topic of the Group Work Circle is defined. If the circle is used to solve an organizational problem, the goal might be to define the problem, to brainstorm alternative solutions, or to reach a decision through consensus. Similar tasks might be used to discuss and resolve a conflict in the group, or to move through successive stages of strategic planning.

Specific Goals

- To brainstorm
- To make group decisions
- To set individual, group, or organizational goals.
- To solve problems
- To resolve conflicts

Developing Individual and Group Awareness

Our emotional and intellectual lives are so complex that we would be devastated if we couldn't discuss our experiences with one another. When we engage in self-observation and contemplation, and then share our thoughts and feelings at a level beyond superficiality, we develop self-awareness. We come to understand ourselves by looking inward and recognizing how we feel, think, and behave in response to people and events around us. When we listen to others do the same — all in an environment of safety — we expand our understanding of others.

Used regularly, the process of the Group Work Circle, coupled with its content (specific discussion topics), provides us with frequent opportunities to observe ourselves and others in action, and to begin seeing how we contribute to the culture of the organization. We become real people to each other. Even someone with whom you thought you had nothing in common is likely to surprise you by exposing an underlying humanity that erases superficial differences and leads to mutual respect.

Encouraging Group Interaction

Relating effectively to others is a challenge we all face. The Group Work Circle brings out and affirms the positive qualities inherent in everyone and allows participants to practice effective modes of communication.

One of the greatest benefits of the Group Work Circle is that it gently forces us to interact. Every Group Work Circle is a real-life experience where we share, listen, explore, plan, and problem solve together. As we interact, we learn about each other and we realize what it takes to relate effectively to other members of the group.

Positive interaction skills are developed through observing how others feel, think, and behave and comparing these observations to our own feelings, thoughts, and behaviors. We begin to recognize what is effective — what works and doesn't work. We identify what others want and need from us in order for the entire organization to achieve its goals.

The Power of Listening

The Group Work Circle provides us with many opportunities to talk while others actively listen. Listening is perhaps the most powerful interaction skill we can develop. Just through the consistent process of sharing in a safe environment, we develop the ability to clarify our thoughts. We are encouraged to go deeper, become more creative, find new directions, and face and solve difficult problems that may at other times be hidden obstacles to progress.

Many of us do not realize that merely listening can be immensely facilitating to the personal development of others. We do not need to diagnose, probe, or problem solve to help people focus attention on their own needs and use the information and insights in their own minds to arrive at their own conclusions. Because being listened to gives people confidence in their ability to positively affect their lives and the life of the organization, listening is certainly the communication skill with the greatest long-term payoff.

Listening communicates two messages: understanding and acceptance. It is based upon our knowing that we are responsible for solving our own problems. We have the data about what is at issue and, if we can draw a solution from that data, we will have grown a step toward responsible stewardship of the organization.

Addressing Organizational Goals

The Group Work Circle allows the group to achieve organization goals through problem solving, decision making, and goal setting more directly than does open-ended, unstructured discussion. By stating the topic or objective up front, we streamline the process. The desired outcome is never in question, so members can focus their energy on the goal and not on issues that waste time, energy, and money.

Imagine two people — one with a map and the other without — separately seeking the same destination. Either may get off track, but only one has a method for immediate self-correction. So it is with the Group Work Circle. The rules and procedure keep members on task, bringing them back when they stray too far from their objective.

How the Group Work Circle Works

> Every great person is always being helped by everybody; for their gift is to get good out of all things and all persons.
>
> *Ruskin*

Life is full of rules, and the Group Work Circle is no exception. Characteristically, members learn to take the rules of the circle very seriously. They are neither difficult to follow nor a threat to anyone's personal style. In fact, by assuring safety, equality, and inclusion, the rules of the Group Work Circle actually remove many hidden roadblocks to productivity and enjoyment. In a group's first few circles, it helps to take a minute to go over the rules. Once the process is smoothly operational, stating the rules is usually no longer necessary. The behavior of the group demonstrates the presence of the rules with striking clarity.

Group Work Circle Rules

* Listen to the person speaking.
* Respect all comments.
* Share the time equally.
* Allow everyone a turn to speak.
* Speak or pass — the choice is yours.

Most of the rules are self-explanatory. Listening means really listening, not mentally rehearsing what you are going to say, not daydreaming. All members of the group receive equal acceptance and respect as do, by extension, their contributions. Since time is usually limited, members are expected to mentally calculate about how much time they have to share. No one is going to interrupt you in the circle; therefore it is your responsibility to stop so that the next person can have a turn. Every member of the group is given the opportunity to speak to a topic at least once. You will never be coerced or pressured to speak, but taking your turn is an absolute right in the Group Work Circle.

Every Group Work Circle has a leader, and leadership is shared. In other words, one member at a time acts as the leader or facilitator, but the person taking that role voluntarily changes from one circle to the next. No one is pressured to lead in the beginning; however, shared leadership is one of the natural outgrowths of the process.

> As a rule of thumb, involve everyone in everything.
>
> *Tom Peters*

It is the leader's responsibility to introduce the topic, and to ensure that the group adheres to the Group Work Circle Procedure and follows the rules. The leader accepts an extra measure of responsibility for being aware of time constraints so that the entire process can be completed without curtailing anyone's right to speak.

Group Work Circle Procedure

- Make sure the ground rules are understood by all members.
- Introduce the topic or state the objective.
- Elaborate if the topic needs clarification.
- Allow time for members to share their thoughts.
- Discuss and summarize conclusions and insights.

The topic of most Group Work Circles is given in the form of a title. For example, "A Time Success Depended on Me" or "A Change I Would Make to Improve This Organization." However, sometimes a circle group will convene to brainstorm solutions to a specific problem or to reach consensus regarding a decision. In these cases, the topic may be stated as an objective. For example, "Our objective today is to decide unit production goals for the next quarter" or "The objective of this circle is to brainstorm ideas for improving communication between staff in customer service and order fulfillment." Regardless of whether you are addressing a topic or an objective, the process is the same.

Elaborating on a topic simply means giving examples and perhaps defining a term or two, so that everyone understands what is expected. Examples demonstrate the value of sharing specific ideas or thoughts, as opposed to generalizations.

Perhaps the trickiest distinction to make as a new circle member or leader involves the differences between the sharing and discussion phases of the circle. These two phases are procedurally and qualitatively different, yet of equal importance. During the sharing phase, circle members voluntarily share their feelings, ideas, and insights concerning the topic. Each person is given an uninterrupted turn while everyone else listens. Only after all members have shared does the leader open up the circle to the give and take of general discussion. The longer you participate in Group Work Circles, the more you will appreciate the benefits of maintaining the integrity of these two phases.

Briefly summarizing at the conclusion of a circle is particularly helpful when the group has been working on a task, such as brainstorming or problem solving. In such cases, someone will usually be asked to take written notes. A quick summary of those notes will help assure everyone's commitment to the circle's outcomes.

When circles are used to facilitate organizational planning and problem solving, they frequently occur as a series. For example, circle groups may be asked to brainstorm a list of ideas and then reach consensus concerning one idea to recommend to the larger group. After various groups have reported out and all recommended ideas have been listed, the circle groups may be asked to reconvene to select the most appropriate and workable suggestion. Later circles may target construction of a plan for implementing the chosen idea. For example, a topic might be, "One Specific Thing I Will Do to Make This Idea Reality."

Creating Your Own Group Work Circle Topics

When the Group Work Circle is used to facilitate planning, problem solving, decision making, or other organizational endeavors, you will frequently find it necessary to create your own circle topics. The task is easy if you keep a few principles in minds.

The purpose of the Group Work Circle is to encourage participants to reflect on their individual experiences, thoughts, feelings, attitudes, knowledge, and beliefs in relation to the topic. Always try to word the topic with this objective in mind.

State the circle topic in the first person, using "I" or "Me." This enables members to involve themselves with the topic immediately at a personal level, without having to wrestle with a translation, or with a decision regarding whose opinion is desired. (Sometimes the "I" or "Me" is understood, but not explicitly stated.)

Generally speaking, it is relatively easy to talk about things past and more difficult to talk about right now. Therefore, if you have the time, your first circle regarding a particular subject might ask members to recall a relevant event, success, problem, solution, etc. from their past experience. Current problems, solutions, and decisions can be dealt with more easily in subsequent circles. For example, the topic, "How I Solved a Difficult Problem" would precede the topic, "A Difficult Problem I'm Facing in My Job Today."

> The main ingredient of stardom is the rest of the team.
>
> *John Wooden*

Word the topic as specifically as you can. Focusing participants on a clear target saves time and prevents group frustration. Free, unguided discussion is fine for cocktail parties, but organizational change doesn't need anything to slow it further. "One Way I Think We Can Streamline the Delivery Scheduling Process" is better than "Something That Needs Improving."

Sample Topics

Here are some examples of topics, both general and planning-related:

General Topics

A Secret Wish I Have
A Special Possession

A Favorite Place
A Place Where I Feel Safe, Serene, and at Peace
What I Think the World Needs To Be a Better Place
A Secret Fear I Have
A Talent or Ability That I Possess
A Time I Stood Up for Something I Believe In
How I React When I'm Angry
Something I Did That Helped Someone Feel Good
How Someone Hurt My Feelings
What I Value Most in a Friend
An Important Person in My Life
Someone Who Trusts Me
What I Think Good Communication Is
A Success I Recently Experienced
Something I Would Like to Achieve in the Next Five Years

Topics Related to Problem Solving
A Problem That This Organization Solved Easily
A Problem That Was Difficult for This Organization to Solve
The Biggest Problem I Think We're Facing in the Area of....
A Roadblock I Think We Face in Implementing This Plan Is...
My Suggestion for Solving This Problem Is...

Topics Related to Decision Making
A Time I Felt Good and Bad About the Same Thing
A Difficult Decision This Organization Must Make
A Decision That Is Working Well
A Decision That Is Not Working
The Greatest Obstacle I See to Making a Decision
One Way I Think We Can Make This Decision More Effective

Topics Related to Goal Setting/Strategic Planning
A Goal I Believe Would Help This Organization
What I Would Like This Organization to Look Like in Five Years
A Specific Objective That Needs to Be Met in the Next Year

One Thing I Can Do to Help This Organization Reach Its Goal

One Thing I Need From Others in Order to Reach This Goal

Topics Related to Needs Assessment

What I Like Best About This Organization

A Change I Would Make to Improve This Organization

The Greatest Need I Have as a Member of This Organization Is...

A System I Think Works Well and Should Be Kept

A System That Doesn't Work and How I Would Change It

Topics Related to Conflict Resolution

A Time I Was Involved in a Conflict

A Conflict That We Resolved Successfully

A Conflict That Is Threatening The Group Now

A Conflict No One Wants to Deal With

One Way I Think We Could Resolve the Current Conflict

A Resolution I Think Might Satisfy Everyone

> We didn't all come over in the same ship, but we're all in the same boat.
>
> *Bernard Baruch*

Topics Related to Brainstorming

My Idea for an Exciting New Program

Something That Can Be Done Today to Make Positive Change

How I Think This Project Can Be Improved

One Way to Make This a Better Functioning Team

A Simple Change I Think Would Improve Working Conditions

COMPREHENSIVE FEEDBACK MODEL

Among the most important data we receive from or give to others is feedback about behavior. Feedback can provide learning opportunities for each of us. What is required is that we use the reactions of others as mirrors in which to observe the consequences of our behavior. Personal data feedback helps to make us more aware of what we do and how we do it, thus increasing our ability to modify and change our behavior and to become more effective in our interactions with others.

To develop and use the techniques of feedback for personal growth, it is necessary to understand certain characteristics of the process. The following is a brief outline of factors that assist us in making better use of feedback, both as givers and as receivers.

1. Focus feedback on the behavior rather than the person.

Refer to what a person does rather than comment on what he or she is. This focus on behavior implies the use of adverbs (which relate to actions) rather than adjectives (which relate to qualities) when referring to a person. Thus we might say a person "talked considerably in this meeting," rather than that the person "is a loudmouth." Talking in terms of personality traits implies that our feedback relates to deeply ingrained qualities that are difficult, if not impossible, to change. Focusing on behavior implies that our feedback is related to a specific situation that can be changed. Hearing comments about behavior is less threatening to the listener than comments about traits.

2. Focus feedback on observations rather than inferences.

Observations refer to what we actually see or hear in the behavior of another person, while inferences refer to interpretations and conclusions made from what we see or hear. In a sense, inferences and conclusions about a person contaminate our observations and cloud the feedback for the other person. Sometimes inferences and conclusions constitute valuable data for the other person; however, they should always be identified for what they are.

3. Focus feedback on descriptions rather than judgment.

Describing a behavior or event is a process of reporting what occurred, while judgment refers to an evaluation in terms of good or bad, right or wrong, nice or not nice. Judgments arise out of a personal frame of reference or values, whereas description represents neutral (as far as possible) reporting.

4. Focus feedback on describing behavior in terms of "more or less" rather than in terms of "either-or."

The "more or less" terminology implies a continuum on which any behavior might fall, stressing quantity, which is objective and measurable, rather than quality, which is subjective and judgmental. For example, participation of a person in a meeting falls on a continuum from low participation to high participation, rather than "good or "bad" participation. When we fail to observe behavior on a continuum, we run the risk of trapping ourselves into thinking in categories, which usually constitutes a serious distortion of reality.

5. Focus feedback on behavior related to a specific situation, preferably to the "here and now," rather than to behavior in the abstract, placing it in the "there and then."

What you and I do is always related in some way to time and place, and we increase our understanding of behavior by keeping it tied to time and place. Feedback is generally more meaningful if given as soon as appropriate after the observation or reactions occur, thus keeping it concrete and relatively free of distortions that come with the lapse of time.

6. Focus feedback on sharing ideas and information rather than on giving advice.

By sharing ideas and information, we leave people free to decide for themselves, in the light of their own goals in a particular situation at a particular time, how to use the ideas and the information. When we give advice, particularly unsolicited advice, we take away their freedom to determine for themselves what is for them the most appropriate course of action.

7. Focus feedback on the exploration of alternatives rather than answers or solutions.

The more we can focus on a variety of procedures and means for the attainment of a specified goal, the less likely we are to accept prematurely a particular answer or solution — which may or may not fit our particular problem. Many of us go around with a collection of answers and solutions for which there are no problems.

8. Focus feedback on the value it may have to the recipient not on the value or "release" that it provides the person giving the feedback.

The feedback provided should serve the needs of the recipient rather than the needs of the giver. Help and feedback need to be given and heard as an offer, not an imposition.

9. Focus feedback on the amount of information that the receiver can use, rather than on the amount that you have and would like to give.

To overload a person with feedback is to reduce the possibility that he or she may use the feedback effectively. When we give more than can be used, we may be satisfying some need for ourselves rather than helping the other person.

10. Focus feedback on appropriate timing and location so that personal data can be received openly and used productively.

The reception and use of personal feedback can bring about many possible emotional reactions. For this reason, be sensitive to when it is appropriate to provide feedback. Excellent feedback presented at an inappropriate time may do more harm than good.

11. Focus feedback on what is said rather than why it is said.

When providing feedback related to something another person has said, focus on the what, how, when, and where of what was said. These are observable characteristics. Focusing on why a person said something takes us from the observable to the inferred, and brings up questions of motive or intent. Though as listeners we may speculate privately about a person's motives (it's hard not to), our speculations should not be part of personal feedback.

Giving (and receiving) feedback requires courage, skill, understanding, and respect for self and others.

ABOUT THE AUTHOR

David Cowan is president of International Training and Development Associates a consulting and executive coaching.

He is also co-founder of the Realization Center, a nonprofit organization dedicated to reawaking leadership that embraces people, values and the best and highest in individual and organizational effectiveness.

Mr. Cowan is also a credentialed professional executive coach. For over twenty-five years he has provided and continues to provide CEO and senior management services to private and public sector organizations of all sizes who want to move to the realms of highest productivity and greatest accomplishment in every endeavor they pursue. His work has propelled leaders and their organizations to high levels of international recognition.

Initially educated as an engineer, he went on to secure degrees in marketing, accounting with a masters degree in business administration.